PRAISE FOR *QUARTER-LIFE CALLING*

"I love this book! Paul Sohn will cause you to think Kingdom thoughts while you are living your life. There is a lot of meat here; don't miss it."

—*Jeremie Kubicek, co-founder of GiANT Worldwide,*
author of 5 Voices *and* 5 Gears

"An indispensable road map to life for Millennials, Paul Sohn's book provides a steady rudder for navigating a quarter-life crisis. This book is like *The Purpose Driven Life* for Millennials. An indispensable partner for the journey."

—*Frances Hesselbein, president and CEO of the*
Frances Hesselbein Leadership Institute

"You don't want to wait until your midlife crisis to think through important questions of calling and career! Read this book to fully embrace your calling and work from your sweet spot."

—*Peter Greer, president & CEO of HOPE International*
and coauthor of 40/40 Vision *and* Mission Drift

"This book is packed with wisdom, practical exercises, and actionable advice to help you design the life you were meant to have. I will be buying a case to give to friends hitting their twenties because it offers a shortcut to a meaningful, successful life."

—*Skip Prichard, CEO of OCLC, leadership insights blogger*

"What is your calling? While Christian discussions of faith, work, and vocation have grown exponentially in recent years, the books and articles have consistently excluded focused attention on Millennials—until now. Written for Millennials by a Millennial, Paul Sohn offers us a careful reading and response to a generation that we deeply need to consider."

—*Matthew Kaemingk, Cascade Fellows Program for Faith, Work, and Calling*

"QUARTER-LIFE CALLING provides a raw and refreshing honesty into the realities of ambitious individuals of any age. Fortunately, Paul compressed a midlife crisis into the first 25 years instead of his first four or more decades. Importantly, he's reaching out to his generation to help them save fifteen years or more of hollow 'happiness' in exchange for a joy-filled life found in bringing expression to one's purpose and living into one's calling."

—*Kevin W. McCarthy, author of* The On-Purpose Person *and* The On-Purpose Business Person

"With experience and wisdom well beyond his years, Paul Sohn is uniquely positioned to deliver an important message at a critical time. QUARTER-LIFE CALLING is a timely book for a generation that is restless to find purpose and meaning. With the voice of a friend but the authority of a mentor, Paul encourages twentysomethings to not settle for the status quo but to find resonance in the sweet spot of your calling."

—*Jenni Catron, leadership coach and author of* The 4 Dimensions of Extraordinary Leadership

"I often say that success in your twenties is more about setting the table than enjoying the feast. With wisdom, insight, and vulnerability, Paul Sohn's new book guides twentysomethings on how to 'set their tables' to experience a life full of purposeful and meaningful success. Instead of asking, 'What do you want to do when you grow up?' Paul Sohn helps readers ask, 'Who do you want to be and why?' If you're on a journey for clarity, identity, and purpose, please take this book with you."

—*Paul Angone, author of* 101 Secrets For Your Twenties

"This is a book for Millennials who want to break free from the rat race—for those who believe they were created for something more. Paul Sohn speaks volumes to twentysomethings, giving them influential, real-world advice for how to find your calling."

—*Brad Lomenick, former president of Catalyst and author of* H3 Leadership

"Paul Sohn has a clear understanding of how to challenge the reader to discover the true meaning of life. QUARTER-LIFE CALLING is a profoundly helpful and insightful text that all young professionals must take in and devour. With outstanding honesty through his personal testimony, pinpointing the truth and reality of modern society, Paul dives into key elements of discovering our sweet spot and inspiring us to find the calling in the world that we live in all for the glory of God."

—*Daniel Park, senior pastor, New Song Church*

"Paul's book is one I wish I'd had coming out of college. It's so level-headed, practical, and lays out such a clear process for thinking through your God-given calling. In my early twenties, I had no idea what I was called or gifted to do. I didn't really know what 'called' or 'gifted' even meant. I didn't understand vocation or purpose. Work was something I did because I needed to. Paul methodically and invitingly sorts all that out. Whether someone is an A-type driven worker or a meandering creative type, QUARTER-LIFE CALLING will be a significant asset to them."

—*Barnabas Piper, author of* Help My Unbelief *and cohost of* 5 Leadership Questions

"Paul Sohn's QUARTER-LIFE CALLING is the right message at the right time. For young people, it's the right message for those seeking a life of significance, because this book points right to the center of God's plan. And it comes at the right time—when young people are making decisions about career and family, many of which will set the trajectory of their life for decades to come. However, what is most powerful about QUARTER-LIFE CALLING is this: Paul is living out this message and helping others to do the same. And that is the best truth of all—tested and tried…and transformational."

—*Marc Fey, author of* The 2:10 Project

"Paul Sohn is accomplished beyond most his age. His new book, QUARTER-LIFE CALLING, is a playbook on how to get a grip and live your life with passion and purpose. While the title targets twentysomethings, I believe the truth in this book is relevant for anyone who is wrestling with questions of identity, destiny, or legacy. Whatever season of life you are in, there is great wisdom here for you."

—*Tami Heim, president and CEO of Christian Leadership Alliance*

"More than any other leader I know, Paul has thought deeply about the importance of young leaders considering the idea of a quarter-life calling. Paul practices an intentionality that shines through in his passion for empowering young leaders."

—*Ben Sand, CEO of Portland Leadership Foundation*

"Every person who's young or young at heart needs to read this. We all face moments in life when what we thought we believed is completely wrong, and this is a book that will guide you out of that confusion and into the clarity that is your calling."

—*Jeff Goins, bestselling author of* The Art of Work

"Much of my life as a leader in Cru has been focused on encouraging and resourcing our staff women to discover who God made them to be and what he created them to do. I want each one to always, at every season of her life, be making her best contribution to our mission. QUARTER-LIFE CALLING will be a great inspirational and practical book to recommend to our young women just launching on their journeys as well those who are farther down the trail."

—*Judy Douglass, Office of the President, Cru*

QUARTER-LIFE
CALLING

On Behalf of everyone here at Trinity Christian Church of Greater Philadelphia, we want to wish you a great congratulation! May the Lord continue to bless your steps and watch over you. Be courageous and followed the path the Good Lord has set for you. Again,

Congratulations!

QUARTER-LIFE CALLING

PURSUING YOUR GOD-GIVEN PURPOSE
IN YOUR TWENTIES

PAUL SOHN

FaithWords

New York Boston Nashville

FaithWords
Hachette Book Group
1290 Avenue of the Americas, New York, NY 10104
faithwords.com
twitter.com/faithwords

Originally published by Paul Sohn in the USA in 2016 with CreateSpace Independent Publishing Platform

First FaithWords edition: April 2017

FaithWords is a division of Hachette Book Group, Inc. The FaithWords name and logo are trademarks of Hachette Book Group, Inc.

The publisher is not responsible for websites (or their content) that are not owned by the publisher.

The Hachette Speakers Bureau provides a wide range of authors for speaking events. To find out more, go to www.hachettespeakersbureau.com or call (866) 376-6591.

LCCN 2016054239

ISBNs: 978-1-4555-4345-8 (paperback), 978-1-4555-4346-5 (ebook)

Printed in the United States of America

LSC-C

10 9 8 7 6 5 4 3 2 1

For my parents, who helped me find my sweet spot.

CONTENTS

PART V
Why Work?

PREFACE

When I was growing up in Canada, I used to sit cross-legged on the rug of my homestay family's living room watching my favorite tennis player, Roger Federer, play on the pristine grass of Wimbledon. For me it was like getting the chance to view Picasso or Michelangelo at work. Every move Roger Federer made was impeccably masterful. His swings seemed effortless as his hands moved with clockwork precision, carving out winners and putting his opponents out of position. Following his serve Federer would land like a cat. His feet always ready, he'd return most any ball with any spin and control or end each point. Whenever I watched Federer play, I couldn't help but question the game. How can someone possibly hit every shot with such beauty and elegance? It seemed as if he knew from the moment the racket hit the ball that it was a winner.

You could see it on his face: he had found his sweet spot.

I was first introduced to tennis in my ninth grade PE class. I became absolutely fascinated by the science of the sport. I spent countless hours every day after school practicing serves, volleys, and strokes with my friends. I only hit the sweet spot one out of ten times that I approached the ball with my racket. But after a few years of playing, I hired a coach who helped me discover my strengths and blind spots. With deliberate practice, I was able to hit aces and control the racket as if it were an extension of my hand.

It wasn't until I was in senior high that I began to consistently hit aces and win passing shots. Every time I would serve an ace and hit fantastic passing shots, I invariably hit the sweet spot of my tennis racket. I felt the vibration in my fingers and heard a beautiful sound when the ball connected with just the right point on the racquet. My heart would jump, and I'd think, *That's it!*

When you hit the sweet spot, you just know.

Our lives have a sweet spot, too: the zone in which God has called us to live to the fullest, energized and hopeful where we find ourselves each day. Living in our sweet spot makes us come alive.

God has designed each of us to do something naturally well and succeed at it. But if you're like 87 percent of people, you probably haven't found out what it is yet. When you're not hitting your sweet spot, you feel the strain, stress, and resistance of not living for what you were made for. Life becomes a daily grind and there's no meaning to your work. You feel that your strengths and gifts are not being used. You don't feel passion for work or life.

During my twenties, I faced a quarter-life crisis: a season of meaningless frustration and uncertainty that led me on a journey to find and live in my sweet spot. This book chronicles my story and outlines the specific, concrete strategies I used to recalibrate my life and live with greater intentionality. Through my experience and what I've learned, I hope to help you do the same.

Along the way God revealed important indicators of my destiny that helped me to increase my odds of hitting more winners—to better understand and live the unique calling He intends for me. In the last few years, I quit a Fortune 50 job to pursue my calling as a leadership coach and consultant. I made necessary endings with certain individuals and communities that were no longer serving me well. Finding my calling led me to make a number of important shifts in life. I am inviting you to join me on this journey to discover your God-given calling, to unleash your potential, and to live every moment of your life in your sweet spot.

INTRODUCTION

So, what's next? What are you going to do after graduation? Do you have a job lined up?

During college, those questions haunted me. I was living my life with an insurmountable pressure to "make it" and make a name for myself.

Whether the question came from friends, family members, professors, or colleagues, I would respond with the same well-rehearsed elevator pitch every time. "My dream is to become the youngest chief human resources officer at a Fortune 500 company, and I'm doing everything in my power to reach that goal."

And it was true. Every day I hustled. In college, I spent countless hours studying, pulling all-nighters to reach the elusive 4.0 GPA. That was my best shot of succeeding and overcoming my fear of being a nobody in this world. I excelled in extracurricular activities, creating new student clubs and leading student government. I knew these were considered good resume builders, plus they were cool experiences. The rest of my hours revolved around perfecting the craft of the resume itself so I could land my dream job.

With every A on a paper or exam, I was inching my way closer and closer to my ultimate dream. Like many up-and-comers do, I visualized myself as a powerful senior executive, in a penthouse overlooking the Manhattan skyline, working with fellow executives at a Fortune 500 company where I was calling the shots and "changing the world."

My persistence paid off. I secured an enviable internship that became a full-time job at the world's largest aerospace company, and I thought it was a major win. I got to sit in important meetings with senior executives and lead transformational company-wide initiatives. I was making more than $75,000 a year at the age of twenty-six. I had one of the best health-care plans in the country, a matching 401(k) plan, and long-term job security.

My friends envied my quick climb into the corporate world, and my family was delighted by my worldly success.

In my new job, I was laser-focused on improving my performance. All of my effort went into developing myself professionally so that I could be a star player at work. I devoured management and leadership books, subscribed to the *Wall Street Journal*, and connected with reputable business leaders to learn about the latest business trends. I developed a detailed, strategic plan for the next five, ten, and fifteen years of my life. I put a plaque on the wall of my bedroom with visuals inspiring me to become the youngest CHRO of a Fortune 500 company.

I had it all figured out.

Everything seemed to be going perfectly except for one thing: I was actually miserable.

Of course, I never admitted this to anyone, even myself. How could I? All my life, I had gone all-in with the hopes of reaching a dream, so much so that my passion and determination actually started to fade. The harder I worked, the more I felt disconnected and disenchanted with my work. I felt like a mindless zombie, drowning in the current of purposelessness. Every day felt like a grind. Work devolved into a monotonous set of thankless tasks. I wondered where my life was leading.

I couldn't help but begin to notice how my growing disenchantment in the workplace negatively impacted my spiritual life. I found myself growing more distant from God. One day I realized that I had become a Sunday Christian. I felt as though my faith had absolutely no bearing on my nine-to-five job. In fact, I began to grow impatient with God and questioned him about my miserable circumstances.

These frustrations led me to face some fundamentally inconvenient questions about my life: Is this what all my hard work and planning amounted to? Why am I here? Does the work I do matter to God? What's my calling and purpose in life? Is this simply a temporary feeling? What is the true meaning of success?

I came across the words of Trappist monk and spiritual master Thomas Merton, and they seemed to express exactly how I felt: "People may spend their whole lives climbing the ladder of success only to find, once they reach the top, that the ladder is leaning against the wrong wall."[1]

I realized that I was working hard for a life I didn't even want.

Every day the feeling of being lost—of leaning on the wrong wall—tormented me. So I began searching for answers. Instead of in the business section, I sought answers on the self-help and motivation shelves of the bookstores. I devoured every book I could find that may point me toward my life's calling. In fact, they were of no help. I began implementing so-called success strategies that promised to help me find my purpose, only to be dragged into a deeper abyss. I only felt more confused and further away from who I sensed I was created to be.

Finally, I called a timeout on life. Enough was enough. Nothing was working. I turned to God and raised my white flag.

One Sunday night, I was trying to get some rest for an early meeting at work the next day. But I couldn't sleep. I began to feel a shortness of breath. My heart started beating at a fast, pounding rate. From head to toe, my body became drenched with sweat. I wondered whether I was truly experiencing a nervous breakdown. Out of desperation I cried out to God, "Please help me! Rescue me from this pit of emptiness. I give up." At that very moment, my life flashed before my eyes the way some describe it happening in a near-death experience. Whether it had been in school, relationships, or my career, everything had been all about me. There had been no place for God at the center of my life. He had simply been my chauffeur, and I had determined the destination.

The very next day, I called my mentor to explain everything that had happened. As my mentor patiently listened to my story, he suggested I read Os Guinness's signature book on finding one's purpose, *The Call*. The book changed my thinking and turned my life upside down, giving me a refreshing perspective on how to view life.

All my life up to this point, I had measured success by material possessions, power, and prestige. But *The Call* showed me a radically different concept of life and success, in which meaning and purpose are gained by discovering and stewarding God's calling in life. This led me to reprioritize my life, challenging me to reevaluate every initiative I was part of with in my work, extracurricular activities, church, and community. As Guinness said, "Calling is the most comprehensive reorientation and the most profound motivation in human experience."[2] These words resonated immediately. I felt I knew this all along but had never read it so succinctly in a sentence. I realized that God wanted me to respond to the call—His call—on my life and live intentionally for Him.

My personal board of directors was instrumental in helping me go through this paradigm shift. They were my spiritual mentors and advisors who prayed with me along my journey. Ignited by a newly consuming passion, I started a journey to discover my calling. I spent the next few years reading dozens and dozens of books on this topic. This shortlist came from many of my mentors, colleagues, and pastors. I read classics from theologians, such as Gordon Smith's *Courage and Calling*; academic leaders, such as Parker Palmer's *Let Your Life Speak*; and entrepreneurs like Jon Acuff's *Start*. They gave me meaningful insights that further challenged my vision of calling and helped me redefine calling for myself.

It wasn't long until the direction of my life started to change. I jumped off the performance-driven, American dream bandwagon and plunged myself into serious soul searching. This began a season of intense introspection and self-growth. I regularly consulted mentors and gleaned and applied key insights from authors and experts while creating a daily habit of meditating on God's words. It was as if these actions served as a compass that pointed to a true north.

I was attempting to align every aspect of my life toward my calling. Every day, I was traveling closer and closer to the sweet spot where I was living intentionally. I gradually felt as if a huge burden had been lifted from my shoulders. I no longer felt compelled to subject myself to the pressures of the world by simply learning to walk in the way in which I was created. I was learning how to swim in the sea of ambiguity and learning to trust God as my ultimate lifeguard.

As a practical way to reinforce my efforts, I created a timetable and outlined all the activities in my life. I wrote down everything that occupied my time. One by one, I dissected each person or thing on my list and asked myself whether this relationship, activity, or commitment helped me grow closer to my calling or detracted from my success. Some of these decisions weren't easy. I had to sever relationships that I had invested in for a long time. I had to end habits that were becoming detrimental to the pursuit of my calling. Whether that was squandering countless hours scrolling down the newsfeed of Facebook and Instagram or binge-watching TV series on Netflix when I was stressed, I made some necessary endings. Soon I had a list with dozens of items that I had to either start or abandon in order to live with greater intentionality.

So, that meant that after four years of working at my job, I did craziest thing a twenty-eight-year-old could. I quit my high-paying Fortune 500 job with great benefits—without having another official job lined up. (I don't recommend up and quitting a job the way I did. Jumping out of an airplane without a parachute is frowned upon in even the most extreme skydiving groups.)

When I shared the news with my co-workers, they were in utter shock. One of my trusted colleagues pulled me aside and said he never met anyone in my age who decided to quit a job at this company. Most people would do everything in their power to stick with this job for their entire career.

It is no understatement that my parents were gravely concerned about my decision. Like any parents would have, they bombarded me with a litany of questions. *How do you plan to make a living? Can you simply wait more and find another viable option? What happens if plan B fails?* I gave my best answers, although I didn't have all the answers. But I was confident, courageous, and resolute. Since my parents had witnessed the dramatic changes in my life over the last few years, I also could sense that deep down they also knew it was time for me to move on.

In a matter of days after quitting my job, I happened to be on the phone with a Facebook friend for the first time. As I shared my story of leaving a handsome job in corporate America to pursue my calling, he deeply empathized with me. In fact, he shared how he was in a similar situation several years ago and decided to leave the Fortune 500 world to pursue his calling.

Before we ended the call, my Facebook friend made an introduction to a fellow Korean American with whom I immediately felt a profound chemistry. He felt like a kindred spirit. Not only were we the same age, but we shared similar cultural backgrounds, personalities, and long-term aspirations. He shared the vision of GiANT Worldwide, and I felt goose bumps. The vision statement was a carbon copy of the vision and calling God has been planting in my heart. My new friend offered me a job to join GiANT Worldwide as a leadership consultant. I never expected a job offer. I asked my new friend to give me a week before I made my decision. Not having all the answers, I knew deep inside this door had been divinely opened and I need to trust God. My family and close friends agreed. A week later I accepted the job, and everything else was history. In hindsight, I could have never predicted how a simple Facebook conversation could have led to a job offer that was so aligned with my calling.

Along my journey, I've realized something about other professionals my age. I've realized that I'm not alone. I'm not unusual. And I'm not even weird. Purpose and meaning are issues that a lot of twentysomethings grapple with. As someone who has struggled with questions of purpose and meaning,

I believe my story will encourage you. You can live intentionally as a twentysomething and choose to be countercultural, to respond to God's call, and to live according to God's rules instead of the world's rules.

————

As a young Christian, maybe you're tormented by these questions:

What does it look like to discover and pursue God's calling?
What are some tools I can immediately use to better discover my calling?
How can I integrate my faith into my everyday work?

If you want to live in your sweet spot, it's time to answer them.

QUARTER-LIFE
CALLING

PART I

THE 30,000-FOOT VIEW

CHAPTER 1

Recalibrating the Meaning of Life

"From vocation to prayer life to Instagram feed, young people today are searching for meaning and fulfillment in all areas of life."

—*David Kim*

Throughout my teens and early twenties, I searched for meaning and purpose in the wrong things—things that left me empty. First, I turned to possessions and wealth. Growing up, I had this dream to live in a five-bedroom house on a golf estate and to drive a Porsche. I remember the first car I drove was an almost-new Mazda 6. It was a beautiful-looking sedan. Within a few months, I grew tired of it and wanted to drive a BMW. But soon after driving a Beamer, I wanted to drive an even better, more expensive car. Or I would acquire the latest gadget, only to find after a few months I needed to get the next big thing. I operated under the motto "Only a little bit more."

John Rockefeller, who was the first American worth more than a billion dollars, was asked how much money it would take to satisfy him. He replied, "Just a little bit more!"

King Solomon of ancient Israel, the richest and wisest man who ever lived, said, "He who loves money will not be satisfied with money, nor he who loves wealth with his income; this also is vanity" (Eccles. 5:10 ESV). I came to the painful conclusion that the pursuit of possessions is a lot like a wild goose chase. The more you possess, the more you want it. There is no end to it.

When possessions failed to give purpose and meaning to my life, I turned to achievement. I always wanted to make a dent in the universe, to make a name for myself.

As a type-A student, I knew I had to differentiate myself in order to reach that goal, and I threw my whole self into achievement. Everything I did was geared toward the advancement of my work. But the more I achieved, the emptier I felt. The fat paycheck, great reputation, and benefits didn't bring any relief and happiness in my life.

During this time, a conversation I had with one of my mentors proved to be life-changing. He asked me how I was doing, and I went on for half an hour talking about all the engagements and initiatives I was leading. My mentor silently listened until he asked me an unexpected question: "Why are you so busy, Paul? What are you trying to prove? Who are you trying to impress?"

I was taken aback, even angered by his question. What did he mean, what am I trying to prove? Who did he think he was to judge me? But after taking a breath and humbly considering his question, I had a powerful revelation: I had been basing my value and identity on my output. In essence, I was a performance addict. My self-worth had been coming from what I accomplished, not who I was. I was driven beyond healthy limitation. Rarely was I able to relax and enjoy life. My mentor then reminded me, "Paul, God is far more interested in who you are than what you do." This was the first time in my life someone gave me permission to be myself. No more façade. No more self-preservation. I felt like a bird set free. Liberated.

MAN'S SEARCH FOR MEANING AND PURPOSE

How will my life turn out? Why am I here and where am I going? What on earth should I do?

These are a few of the biggest and most common existential questions twentysomethings face. I have asked these questions. We are a generation thirsty for meaning. We want to know that our lives matter, that life is not an accidental by-product of nature, a result of matter plus time plus chance. Rather, our lives were creatively designed and have built-in meaning, purpose, and hope.

A survey from *USA Today* asked, "What would you ask a God or Supreme Being if you could get a direct and immediate answer?" The highest percentage (34 percent) of people said they would ask, "What is my purpose in life?" Barna Group's research found that an overwhelming 87 percent of Millennials surveyed want to find a life full of meaning.[1] Further, Millennials don't just work for a paycheck, according to another survey by Gallup. First and foremost, they want a purpose.

In comparison, meaning wasn't something Baby Boomers needed to derive from their jobs. They found that in their families and communities. Their focus was right in front of them. Whereas, arguably, Millennials are influenced by the technological age in which we live. We're connected by technology, better enabled to envision ourselves in relation to a global community. Our perspective is widened, if not also more fixed on ourselves, if we're not careful. Millennials want to achieve a greater purpose beyond a simple paycheck. They desire to work for organizations with impact and to believe in the mission of the organization— they want make a dent in the universe. And they can.

One of the most important books I've ever read is Viktor

Frankl's *Man's Search for Meaning*. In September 1942, Viktor Frankl, a prominent Jewish psychiatrist and neurologist in Vienna, was arrested and transported to a Nazi concentration camp with his wife and parents. Three years later when his camp was liberated, most of his family, including his pregnant wife, had perished—but he, prisoner number 119104, had lived. Frankl concluded that the difference between those who had lived and those who had died came down to one thing: the presence or lack of meaning.[2]

They were not living in their sweet spot.

The search for meaning and purpose is universal. But we miss it when we measure our lives based on the wrong things: material possessions like expensive cars, temporal pursuits, and passing fads—things that do not deliver true meaning and fulfillment. They may bring immediate gratification, but the euphoria dies down and is replaced by an even greater yearning for true meaning.

RETHINKING HOW YOU MEASURE YOUR LIFE

Harvard Business School professor Clayton Christensen opens his book *How Will You Measure Your Life?* with a disturbing story. He describes the surprising changes that he witnessed every five years at the reunions of a prestigious business school. At his fifth-year reunion, he notices how successful people were. Many of his classmates were quickly rising up the highest rungs in the corporate ladder in companies like McKinsey and Company and Goldman Sachs. He thought, "Their lives seemed to be destined to be fantastic on every level."[3]

But around the tenth-year reunion, Christensen notices an uncommon pattern:

A number of my classmates whom I had been looking forward to seeing didn't come back, and I had no idea why. Gradually, by calling them or asking other friends, I put the pieces together... Behind the façade of professional success, there were many who did not enjoy what they were doing for a living. There were, also, numerous stories of divorces or unhappy marriages.[4]

Surely, Christensen thought, this was a blip, an inevitable midlife crisis, but he was dead wrong. At the ensuing twenty-five and thirty-year reunions, the problems worsened. Many of his classmates were experiencing family failure, personal dissatisfaction, even criminal behavior. In fact, one of his classmates— Jeffrey Skilling, former CEO of Enron—ended up in jail for his role in the Enron scandal.

What was going on? Obviously, these men and women didn't plan their way to failure. At the surface, these were the movers and shakers in the corporate world, but only a little digging would show that something went wrong along the way.

Christensen finally asked the ultimate question: "How will you measure your life?"

Like Christensen's classmates, many twentysomethings measure success or progress in life against how fast and how high they are climbing the career ladder. Their belief that prestigious titles and hard work will provide them the happiness they pursue turns out to be misleading.

One of the clients I coach is a young and ambitious twenty-three-year-old who often reminds me of myself when I was his age. Graduating at the top of his class from a reputable university, he ended up working in a growing start-up tech firm. After a year, he felt a growing disillusionment because he wasn't experiencing a fast enough climb up the corporate ladder. Only by asking himself tough, deep questions did he uncover that much of his identity was rooted in the external, including his accomplishments, title, and salary and the perceptions of others. For most of his life, he thought these were the tools he needed to use to make a name for himself and convince others that he is worthy. The more we talked this through, my client realized how faulty this thinking is, and he shifted his desire to find purpose and meaning in something else, something designed by his Creator.

EVERYTHING WAS MEANINGLESS

I read a story about Michael Jordan and felt an interesting connection. When he turned fifty, *ESPN the Magazine* ran an extended interview about Jordan's continuing obsession with the best days of his basketball career. The article stated:

> [Jordan's] self-esteem has always been, as he says, "tied directly to the game." Without it, he feels adrift. Who am I? What am I doing? For the past 10 years, since retiring for the third time, he has been running, moving as fast as he could, creating distractions, distance. When the schedule clears, he'll call his office and tell them not to bother him for a month, to let him relax and play golf. Three days later they'll get another call, asking if the plane can pick him up and take him someplace. He's restless...He feels his competitiveness kick in, almost a chemical thing, and he starts working out, and he wonders: Could he play at 50? What would he do against LeBron?...

> [Jordan asks], "How can I enjoy the next 20 years without so much of this consuming me? How can I find peace away from the game of basketball?"[5]

I often felt like this as I feverishly pursued my meaning in worldly success instead of seeking it in relation to God, the Author and Creator of life. How could I let go of the control I felt while clinging to my plans and professional security? I came to a point when I had no choice but to try. I had to consider that perhaps how I had defined success wasn't how God defined success. I realized I needed to do a lot of difficult unlearning, unraveling, and demystifying of the lies I had bought into all my life. It was a time to redefine my values according to God's perspective to see what is truly in store for me.

And God led me out of my quarter-life crisis and into my quarter-life calling.

QUESTIONS FOR REFLECTION AND DISCUSSION

1. How would you answer the question "How do you measure your life?"

2. By what standards are you currently measuring your life?

3. Are there things by which you measure your life and worth that make you feel empty?

4. Do you have perceptions that need to be reconsidered? Could they be preventing you from living intentionally toward your calling?

CHAPTER 2

Whole-Life Stewardship

"Success and failure are master words; faithfulness is the concern of stewards."

—*J. D. Greear*

I grew up believing in the dangerous myth called the American Dream. That is, if I put in the hard work, I could be anything I wanted to be. The world shouts, "Pursue your passions! Dream big! You can be the very best in what you do." I deceived myself into thinking I could become the next Steve Jobs, Mark Zuckerberg, or Taylor Swift of the world. Success was all about competing—and I wanted to win. It was about who had the most power, prestige, popularity, and possessions.

I had virtually everything I thought I wanted in my midtwenties. A good salary that afforded an apartment with a jaw-dropping, panoramic view of downtown Portland. A Fortune 50 brand on my resume with incredible potential to climb the corporate ladder. A company that invested in my leadership development and further continuing education. A beautiful girlfriend who always had my back. But I still found myself thoroughly wanting. While my unquenchable desires grew to a crescendo each day, I found myself developing unnerving restlessness, despair, and frustration.

I was basing my beliefs and values on the wrong things: Money. Titles. Power. Temporal and fleeting things that would evaporate when I die.

Instead of succumbing to what the world wanted of me, I was prompted to listen to what my Creator wanted in my life. I needed to go through a complete makeover. I needed to redefine how I viewed success based on what Scripture teaches.

Like a miner searches for gold, I spent several months diving into the Scriptures every day, looking for how God truly defined success. When I encountered the story of the parable of the talents, I knew this was it. The story radically reoriented my view of success.

THE PARABLE OF THE TALENTS

In the gospel of Matthew, the parable of the talent illustrates a powerful story about how Jesus defines success. The parable of the talents teaches that the kingdom of heaven will be like a man going on a long voyage. Before he leaves, he gives five talents (a large unit of money) to the first servant, two talents to the second, and one talent to the third. Here talents represent a very large sum of money, perhaps millions in today's currency. Two of the servants earn 100 percent returns by trading with the funds, but the third servant hides the money in the ground and earns nothing. The rich man rewards the two who made money but severely punishes the servant who invested nothing.

As we consider this parable, we can interpret talents as resources that God has endowed us with, whether it be time, abilities, or treasure.

God has a simple standard for measuring success. In His

kingdom, success in life is about stewardship and maximizing what we've been given. God calls us to be faithful stewards.

As a Lean Practitioner at Boeing, I was able to employ stewardship. In fact, I considered my main job function to be one of a steward. My key concern was to evaluate how people were using their time, talent, and resources, and to make necessary changes to maximize the efficiency of airplane production. For instance, I examined the number of days it took us to produce a jet, and I would work with teams to see if that number could be cut in half. The question I was always asking was "How can we make the same airplane in less time for less money?" By working with shop floor team members, we generated productive ideas and solutions to best steward our time, skills, and resources to create a better product. However, not all meetings with shop floor members were constructive, as some didn't possess a vital stewardship mentality but simply viewed their work as a means to a paycheck and never wanted to improve.

I like the way the Bible describes stewardship as a profound understanding that we're not the principal owners of our lives, but managers. Psalm 24:1 (NLT) declares that "the earth is the LORD's, and everything in it." Therefore, the responsibility of a twentysomething Christian is the God-given privilege to manage a part of God's property. In this way, we are stretching ourselves to leverage our abilities, rather than letting them stagnate. Without this perspective, everything we engage in is for the glory of the self, not God. With a true perspective of stewardship, everything is for the glory of God.

When you hear the word *stewardship*, you might quickly

grab your wallet either to open it or to hold it more firmly closed. We often equate stewardship as tithing or caring for the environment. But the essence of stewardship is greater than that. Whole-life stewardship involves every choice we make in our lives. In the words of Ron Blue, the essence of stewardship is the "use of God-given resources for the accomplishment of God-given goals."[1] Stewardship means that we are not owners, but simply managers or administrators.

I believe that only through stewardship can someone achieve true success and live a life worth living. As the apostle Paul says, "Moreover, it is required of stewards that they be found faithful" (1 Cor. 4:2 ESV). Paul knew that he would account for the time, talent, and treasure he'd be given by God. The issue is faithfulness. While the word *success* is rarely used in the Scriptures, the word *faithful* is used throughout the Bible. Here are several examples from the Bible:

- "Well done, good and faithful servant!" (Matt. 25:21 NIV)
- Those who have been given a trust must prove faithful. (1 Cor. 4:2 NIV)
- A faithful person will be richly blessed. (Prov. 28:20 NIV)
- "The Lamb will triumph over them because he is Lord of lords and King of kings—and with him will be his called, chosen and faithful followers." (Rev. 17:14 NIV)

What God requires of you is not success, but faithfulness in your calling. Ask yourself, "What has God called me to do?" In what areas in my life can I faithfully steward my time, talent, and treasure so I can become the best version of myself? You aren't called to change the world, but you are called to follow Jesus in every situation. This requires intentionality, clarity, and focus. Will you choose to steward or squander your life?

When we define our success according to the quality of our stewardship, this frees us to be ourselves. For a steward, success in life is knowing what God has called you to and being completely faithful to it. When you say yes to Christ, you are comfortable saying no to others. We don't need to strive to be something we're not. I have learned that life doesn't need to be a competition. It's about becoming the best versions of ourselves. Stewarding our calling inevitably requires us to muster up the courage to say no to the expectations of the world but yes to our Caller. This knowledge has helped me achieve peace and a much greater understanding of my purpose.

Bill Peel, executive director of the Center for Work and Faith, said, "Although God gives us 'all things richly to enjoy,' nothing is ours. Nothing really belongs to us. God owns everything; we're responsible for how we treat it and what we do with it. While we complain about our rights here on earth, the Bible constantly asks, 'What about your responsibilities?' Owners have rights; stewards have responsibilities."[2]

When I was a college freshman, I borrowed my friend's luxury car for a few days. When I drove him back to his house, I wanted to impress him with my *Fast and Furious*–like driving skills. I hit the accelerator hard when a stoplight turned green and left a pretty good amount of rubber on the pavement. My friend, who was utterly shocked by my actions, said, "I made a big mistake lending you my car. Get out of the seat, because

I'm driving from now on." It dawned on me that I should have been a good steward of my friend's property. Instead of abusing my friend's car, I should have taken great care of what he had entrusted me with. That was the last time my friend ever lent me his car.

Likewise, Colossians 3:23 points out that we have a responsibility to exercise stewardship over the God-given resources in our lives. Just like the car I borrowed from my friend, the resources do not belong to us. We were given the privilege and authority to be God's stewards of his calling in our lives.

The truth is that no other period in our lives will be more impacted by the choices we make than our twenties. In our twenties we may choose what grad school to attend, what job to take, where to live, what person to marry, and what activities to volunteer for. And stewardship ultimately drives our entire decision-making process.

IT'S NOT ABOUT YOU

Consider the opening lines of Rick Warren's *The Purpose Driven Life*: "It's not about you."[3] True stewards clearly understand that they are not the owners of their life, but managers. This was one of the most transformative realizations I ever made.

Leading up to my internal crisis of meaning, I had been asking the wrong questions. It had been all about me, me, me: What am I supposed to do with my life? What do I want to be? What are my goals, my ambitions, my vision for my future? I was the acting captain of my soul, the master of my fate. Even as a Jesus follower, there had been no place for God in my ship, my dream, or my life. I was the commander, God the first mate.

I never asked where He wanted to steer. I never asked where He wanted to go. And I now know that I was mistaken.

DYING TO SELF

In a world where everything seems to be about you—loving yourself, promoting yourself, taking care of yourself, and protecting yourself—Jesus says otherwise: crucify yourself. The world clamors to live for the self, but God's Word asks us to die to the self. It's a big commitment with the greatest of rewards. But although many people approached Jesus to become His disciples, most of them turned away. Unfortunately they were unwilling to give their entirety to Christ.

But you see, only in dying to ourselves do we truly find ourselves. That's the greatest paradox of redefining success. Jesus said, "Self-help is no help at all. Self-sacrifice is the way, my way, to finding yourself, your true self" (Matt. 16:25 THE MESSAGE). The apostle Paul also wrote, "Obsession with self in these matters is a dead end; attention to God leads us out into the open, into a spacious, free life" (Rom. 8:6 THE MESSAGE).

Discovering your calling requires you to die to yourself. You must surrender yourself totally and completely to our Creator, our Audience of One.

As Max Lucado rightly said, "Don't go to God with options and expect him to choose one of your preferences. Go to him with empty hands—no hidden agendas, no crossed fingers, nothing behind your back. Go to him with a willingness to do whatever He says. If you surrender your will, then He will equip you with everything good for doing His will."[4]

When God revealed His glory to Isaiah, the prophet offered

himself completely (Isa. 6:8). Paul submitted his whole self to Christ on the Damascus road (Acts 9:15–19). Even Jesus, our ultimate example, daily surrendered to His Father's will (John 5:19). A life of surrender says, "God, whatever, whenever, wherever, and however you want it, my answer is yes."

The ultimate reward of death to self and daily cross bearing is intimacy with Christ. When we seek the face of God and make Him our everything, we truly find who we are and why we were created. We end up marching to a different drummer. Rather than following the demands and expectations of the world, we ought to ask God what He wants in our lives first and foremost. We should ask, "What do you want me to be? What is the reason why you created me? Will you show me what to do?" When it becomes God-directed instead of self-directed, our life suddenly takes on a true sense of meaning and purpose.

STEWARDING YOUR CALLING

I think that every one of us has a unique calling from God. Unfortunately, only 40 percent of Christians feel that they have a clear sense of what it is.[5] It wouldn't surprise me if the stats were much lower for twentysomething Christians who are still figuring out who they are, where they are going, and why they were created.

Calling always requires choice and courage—that is, to either accept God's call and live obediently and intentionally, or to reject His call and fail to steward our God-given potential. We have been endowed with particular gifts, desires, and opportunities. We can choose to maximize our resources to live out our calling or simply squander these resources on ourselves. The truth is, when we live our lives according to our calling and where we know God is leading us, we become a rare commodity in this noisy world.

EXERCISE: STEWARDING GOD'S CREATION

The purpose of this exercise is to cultivate a mindset of stewardship as it relates to God's creation and environment.

1. Take a stroll around your neighborhood. Assess the ground, the pavement, the sky, the buildings, the plants/trees, and the garbage. If the neighborhood is in a city or town, consider a trip to a more rural area.

2. Read Psalm 8.

3. Make two columns for journaling on a page, titling them "The world as it should be" and "The world as it shouldn't be but is."

4. Fill the appropriate columns with your observations.

5. Then, discuss some of the following questions with family and friends:

   - Why is the world as it shouldn't be?

   - Why should we care about the environment and God's creation?

   - What does looking after God's creation have to do with God? (Gen. 1:1; James 4:8a)

6. Make a list including some of your daily actions for a week. Ask yourself: How does each action hurt or help God's earth and environment? How can I be a better steward of these things in the world around me?

QUESTIONS FOR REFLECTION AND DISCUSSION

1. What things in your life have always been about you instead of about God?

2. What is preventing you from adopting a mindset of stewardship?

3. How does the idea of stewardship of calling impact your view of success?

PART II

THE TWENTYSOMETHING TRANSITION

CHAPTER 3

The Quarter-Life Crisis

"This is a generation hungry for substantive answers to life's biggest questions, particularly in a time when there are untold ways to access information about what to do. What's missing—and where the Christian community must come in—is addressing the how and why."

—*David Kinnaman*

Some of you feel disillusioned with your entry-level salaries, which seem too insignificant to pay off your student loans—or even pay the electric bill. Some of you graduate from college only to find your degree too specialized, making it impossible to find a job in a related field. Or you may have moved to a new city for a new job and found yourself lost in the masses, struggling to adjust to the new environment. Some of you are still undecided on your career path and feel like you're just existing instead of living to your fullest. Or you feel you can't afford to think about your purpose and calling—you're hustling every day to survive and make your ends meet. Finding your calling sounds too good to be true.

Welcome to the world of "adultolescence." Today most twenty-somethings, a generation 80 million strong, live with a staggering and unprecedented amount of fear, uncertainty, and hopelessness.

Several decades ago, a majority of men and women completed all the major transitions into adulthood by age thirty: leaving home, finishing school, becoming financially independent, getting married, and having a child. Today, less than half of men and women complete these transitions by age thirty.[1] According to a national survey, eighteen- to twenty-four-year-olds report that gaining a clear sense of your purpose in life is an integral part of becoming a "real" adult. Nearly 90 percent of twentysomethings say that making life decisions aligned to their purpose makes them an adult. But only 43 percent say they have a clear sense of what they desire in life, 36 percent say their career path intersects with their purpose, and only 30 percent know why they are here.[2]

———————

Most of my young adult life, I strove to follow a linear path. Get into a good high school. Get good grades. Get into a top-ranked college. Get good grades. Get involved in student clubs. Lead student government. Graduate as a top student. Find a reputable job. Live my dreams.

My life looked so good on paper. But a growing feeling of disappointment overwhelmed me. I wondered, "Is this all there is?" The job I thought would bring me fulfillment—in my mind, at least—turned out to be less glamorous, less fulfilling, and less meaningful. In fact, it was toxic in many ways. The result was an overwhelming sense of helplessness and cluelessness.

Many times, instead of a twentysomething I felt like a "twentynothing." As opposed to feeling like I was living an exciting and prosperous period of my life, in my twenties I battled a sense of inferiority and felt like I was drifting into nothingness. My accomplishments could never be grand enough to fulfill me. It was my quarter-life crisis—a "period of anxiety, uncertainty, and inner turmoil that often accompanies the transition to adulthood."[3]

FIVE KEY FACTORS THAT MAY CAUSE YOU TO ENTER INTO A QUARTER-LIFE CRISIS

1. Fear and Anxiety

"Our greatest fear should be not of failure, but of succeeding at something that doesn't really matter."
—*Author Unknown*

You may be in your twenties but feel like you're in your forties. The world says you are young and should be having the time of your life, but all you can think of is the overwhelming sense of stress, career prospects, and scary debts.

Will my college education have any value after graduation? Will I ever earn enough money to buy a house? How can I think about marrying and having kids when my job security is so uncertain that I don't know if I can afford myself in a year? These are a few of the authentic questions we face in our twenties.

In their book *Repacking Your Bags*, Richard Leider and David Shapiro found that the number one fear of most people is to have lived a meaningless life.[4] Twentysomethings live in a generation that has seen an increasingly high rate of turnover due to layoffs and technological explosion, which changes the dynamics of the job market. The employment rate of eighteen- to thirty-one-year-olds in 2012 was only 63 percent. Even those who have a college degree are struggling to find a job, with the rate of unemployment of twentysomethings holding a BA degree or higher jumping from 7.7 percent to a little over 13 percent in 2012.[5]

These changes are forcing twentysomethings to pursue more education instead. All of these factors create a staggering amount of uncertainty. Today, we live in a world where change is the only constant. In fact, twentysomethings experience more change than their predecessors. We move back in with parents, change jobs, change cities, change churches. Exploring our identity and the instability in our lives are unfortunately the two sides of the same coin. One doesn't exist without the other.

2. The Choice Overload and FOMO

Millennials face a larger variety of choices and options than any other generation. They are overburdened with choices. In fact, having too many options can have a paralyzing effect.

The explosion of options is something that has only occurred in the last fifty years. Many people in underdeveloped economies who live on a dollar a day simply do not have the freedom and opportunity to make many choices. The same is true of our grandparents. Most likely, you either inherited your parents' farm or followed your father's trade. The choices in life were a lot simpler.

On the other hand, you will likely have ten to twelve jobs over your lifetime, including three or four different careers. You may be bombarded with endless opportunities. You may be able to go to any school you want, major in hundreds of different topics, live almost in any place in the world, and have a chance to connect with almost any person on social media. We have millions of choices ranging from what clothes to wear, what music to listen to, what shows to watch, which social networks to engage in, which people to be friends with, which game to play, which TV station to watch, which college to attend, which major to study, which job to have, which car to drive, who to date, when to get married, where to live, and the list goes on.

It's overwhelming.

This overload of choices is accentuated by a recent phenomenon called fear of missing out (FOMO). Twentysomethings live in a culture that is online and plugged in 24/7. We live in an era where we're accosted by the incessant sharing of meals, vacations, parties, and sheer awesomeness people are experiencing—thanks to Facebook, Twitter, and Instagram. According to a new study by Eventbrite, 69 percent of Millennials experience FOMO when they can't attend something that their family or friends are going to. "For Millennials, FOMO is not just a cultural phenomenon, it's an epidemic," the report reads.[6]

Each time you log into Instagram and witness the activities of others, you might be thinking, "I wish I was doing that." With FOMO, you want to be everywhere doing everything. The issue that has arisen in this social media age is that you're actually able to be everywhere and nowhere at the same time. All of the options before you lead to choice overload and the dreaded FOMO.

On the surface, having lots of choices sounds appealing, as it seems to equate to greater freedom. We think more choices can make us happy. But instead, too many options can actually be debilitating. We can become frozen with indecision, even suffer decision fatigue, trying to constantly weigh our options in every area of our lives.

3. The YOLO Generation

You only live once. Have fun while you can. Enjoy every minute. Every day. Spend $100 today instead of investing $100 in the future. Buy the new outfit now and pay the credit card bill later. You only have one life, for God's sake.

YOLO is the motto for many who are part of the social media generation. The average millennial spends eighteen hours a day consuming media—often in multiple forms at once. They also check their smartphone forty-three times and spend nearly five and a half hours on social media per day.[7]

You are part of a generation that lives, eats, and breathes social media. In fact, social media makes it seem rather countercultural to think about the next five, ten, or fifteen years. Twentysomethings are geared toward living in the present, for the present, and they often find themselves experiencing "living with the present bias." That is, we live our lives as if we have an infinite amount of life. For many, the philosophy of "you only live once" is not sufficient motivation for meaningful, purposeful living. Rather, it can become convenient justification for fun but reckless living. Many twentysomethings have grown up in a culture obsessed with instant gratification and self-absorption, and the promotion of short-term thinking can make it hard to envision the future clearly and lead to irrevocable regrets later in life.

4. Too Busy to Slow Down

"Busyness can be a way to avoid God, the meaning of life, and life itself."

—*Sidney S. Macaulay*

This generation is part of a 24/7 society. Overscheduled. Overworked. Overwhelmed. Overcommitted. Twentysomethings are always busy, scurrying, doing something. But we have to consider the value of the actions consuming our time.

We live in a world that values *doing* more than *being*. Studies show that between the ages of fifteen and eighty-eight, more than four in ten Christians around the world say they "often" or "always" rush from task to task. About six in ten Christians say that it's "often" or "always" true that "the busyness of life gets in the way of developing my relationship with God."[8]

We are too busy focusing on schoolwork, extracurricular activities, and launching our careers. When we enter our jobs, we work more hours than ever. The average workweek is now up to forty-seven hours, four more hours a week than two decades ago. And a Gallup poll found that 44 percent of Americans call themselves "workaholics."[9]

The problem is that busyness is deafening. When we're overly busy, we fail to hear to the voice of God. Discovering our calling requires us to be on the same frequency with Him. With the deluge of to-dos that controls our lives, we begin to walk without direction.

Even busywork for God can cause us to stumble and distract us from finding our calling. Oswald Chambers urged, "The greatest competitor of devotion to Jesus is service for Him.... The one aim of the call of God is the satisfaction of God, not a call to do something for Him."[10] It's so easy to be preoccupied with our work that we actually lose our ability to hear God's voice in the midst of it. Even if our activities are intended as service to Him, yet they overwhelm our minds, they can drown out His call in our lives and lead us toward a quarter-life crisis.

5. The Obsessive Comparison Disorder

I lived for a good part of my childhood in South Korea—we moved to the US when I was three, but moved back to Seoul for five years when I was nine. There it was survival of the fittest. I was a number, competing with other numbers, in order to ace those exams. I was called upon more by my number than my real name. That was who I was.

My identity was dependent upon my letter grade. The better I did, the more superior I felt, but the worse I did, the more I felt a deep sense of shame. When I looked around, I always found people who were better than me at something. I admired their abilities and strengths and always felt inadequate. Sure, I wanted to have Bill Gates's wealth, Taylor Swift's popularity, Albert Einstein's brains, Walt Disney's imagination, and Mother Teresa's heart all at one time. I wanted it all. I was hostage to my comparison reflex.

Millennial expert Paul Angone calls this obsessive comparison disorder (OCD). He says, "OCD is the smallpox of our generation."[11] This is an epidemic that is producing unwanted thoughts and feelings, driving us into depression, consumption, anxiety, and all-around discontent. We think the grass is always greener on the other side. You might need to hear this again, so let me say it once more: it's not greener on the other side.

Just look at Facebook or Instagram, where the achievements of others are endlessly and strategically promoted. It might look like most of your high school friends are getting engaged, having children, or buying new cars and houses while you're still just trying to get by as an adult.

The media fosters a detrimental comparison mindset. If you're a twentysomething woman in America, you see about three thousand advertisements each day—many of which convey messages about what the "ideal" female body should look like.[12] The truth is, 98 percent of American women are not as thin as the fashion models who supposedly have the "right" body type. The average American woman is five-foot-four and weighs 165 pounds. The average Miss America winner is five-foot-seven and weighs 121 pounds. Nearly 20 million women currently living in the United States will suffer from an eating disorder at some point in their lives[13]—possibly a consequence of obsessive comparison disorder.

We need to make sure we don't spend our lives trying to be people we were not meant to be. Imagine God, the Creator and Author of our lives, looking at His creation and seeing us waste all our time trying to please the world and be people we were not created to be. And the result is that His people, who are intended for an amazing purpose in Him, are stuck in disappointment, a deep abyss, nothing but emptiness. What a waste. We yearn to be whole, and we only will be when we find our confidence in who God created us to be.

THANK GOD FOR A QUARTER-LIFE CRISIS

I am thankful I have experienced a quarter-life crisis. What was the most turbulent and confusing time of my life became one of the best things to happen to me. My quarter-life crisis brought about incredible clarity to help me find my quarter-life calling. It gave me the courage and vision to quit a Fortune 50 job to pursue my calling. My quarter-life crisis led me to surrender my ego and learn to trust that God has plans greater than I ever imagined. Now, I get to live in my sweet spot and live out my calling as a leadership consultant, author, and speaker.

I am also grateful that through my experience I am able to help you. Now that you know the five key factors that lead to a quarter-life crisis, I hope you will examine them in relation to your own life, so that you can guard against them and be more equipped to live intentionally.

This is a time to embrace ambiguity. This is a time to explore life, so you won't be lost later. This is a time to understand how your failures, uncertainties, and fears point to the Author and Creator of everything who provides the meaning of your existence, and can help you to find your purpose in life. If you feel like you're on a perpetual hamster wheel, feel lost, or are going through a similar crisis of faith and identity as I was, read on—you're about to discover how to find your calling.

EXERCISE: STOP DOING LIST

Practice the art of creating a stop-doing list. A stop-doing list encourages you to identify habits, behaviors, and thoughts that kill your dreams. Create a list of ten things you should stop doing.

1. _____

2. _____

3. _____

4. _____

5. _____

6. _____

7. _____

8. _____

9. _____

10. _____

QUESTIONS FOR REFLECTION AND DISCUSSION

1. Which of the five factors that contribute to a quarter-life crisis do you struggle with the most?

2. How do you deal with fear and anxiety in your life?

3. What happens when you have no time to slow down?

4. What causes you to compare yourself to others?

CHAPTER 4

Discovering Your True Identity

"We cannot consistently behave in ways that are different from what we believe about ourselves."

—*Kenneth Boa*

One of my favorite movies is *Memento*. The lead character, Leonard Shelby, is on a mission to hunt down his wife's killer. His search is derailed when he gets a blow to the head by the murderer, resulting in anterograde amnesia, a condition that makes it impossible to remember anything new for more than a few minutes.[1]

In order to cope with his memory loss, Leonard creates a complex system using notes, tattoos, and Polaroid photos to remember certain facts regarding his wife's murder. Throughout the movie, several people try to manipulate and exploit Leonard's condition for their own benefit. As the movie progresses, viewers begin to wonder if Leonard is the true Leonard as the movie portrays.

In one defining scene, Teddy, Leonard's manipulative "friend," says to Leonard, "You don't know who you are anymore."

"Of course I do," Leonard replies. "I'm Leonard Shelby. I'm from San Francisco."

"No, that's who you were," Teddy says. "Maybe it's time you started investigating yourself."

What follows is a series of revelations about Leonard, which leads him to doubt his identity and question the system he's built. Consequently, he suffers a severe identity crisis.

Like Leonard Shelby, many of us wrestle with coming to know our true identity. Throughout my twenties, I wrestled with mine. I felt lost. I grew restless. I knew I was supposed to be living in my life's most transformative period of self-discovery. I was at a crossroads. I could either use that time to learn more about how God designed me or continue to be like Shelby, manipulated by false, competing voices.

A few years ago, I participated in a simple exercise at a leadership development program at work. The instructions were clear: write down all the of the attributes that I could think of for myself. After a few hours of thinking and writing, I ended up with over fifty attributes. Surprisingly, I was more confused about myself after this exercise. I wondered whether all fifty of these attributes were really defining characteristics of my identity. As I asked many of my friends and family, they didn't relate many of the attributes I had listed to me. I realized that many of the attributes I had written down were attributes I didn't have but strongly desired to have. In hindsight, I know I was trying to be somebody I wasn't, somebody that everybody wants to be. I was trying to function as a toaster when I was created to be a blender. In my confusion I ultimately became neither and ended up becoming a product nobody really wants to buy, one without a clear purpose.

Max Lucado perfectly describes this type of misguided thought in *Cure for the Common Life*: "We suffer from poor I-sight. Not eyesight, a matter of distorted vision that lenses can correct, but I-sight. Poor I-sight blurs your view, not of the world, but of yourself."[2]

A NOISY WORLD

You live in a noisy world. A myriad of voices seek to influence how you view yourself. You can easily be drowned by these competing voices, drifting away from the one true voice. Many of these voices prevent you from knowing who you really are and make you question your identity in Jesus Christ. What you struggle with is how often these voices masquerade as truths.

Much of the prevailing mindset of our generation is influenced by Hollywood and the surrounding culture. These messages from the media work to convince you that you desperately need a certain product or service. If you don't get it, you are missing out. These voices say you are fat. You are ugly. You need the latest gadgets to make you happy. Sex, lust, and immorality are perfectly acceptable as long as you are honest and responsible.

The American culture celebrates the American Dream. Its motto says, "I can be anything I want to be if I put in the hard work." Contrary to what our culture tells us, I cannot be anything I want to be; I can only be the best version of who I was created to be. As long as you're unsure of who you are in Christ, you're going to be pressured to fit into other people's expectations. They will manipulate you. They will force you to make decisions that often go against the Word of God.

Not only does the media have an impact on our view of life, but some of the most influential voices are those of our parents. I was raised under "tiger parents" who, like many other Asian parents, were overly strict with their children by restricting free time to focus on achieving the highest grades. While my mom was a more relaxed tiger mom, she was a tiger mom nonetheless.

Growing up in a hypercompetitive environment in Korea, education was everything. My tiger mom understood the value of education and how it became a means of survival and societal advancement. I was constantly bombarded by messages that I didn't measure up or that I wouldn't amount to anything with my grades. Slow learner. Inefficient. Unproductive. The incessant impression that I needed to succeed and follow in the footsteps of my dad overwhelmed me.

Early childhood experiences often lead twentysomethings away from discovering their true identity. In your upbringing, you may have been wounded by people during this emotional period of life. Maybe you experienced substantial trauma, including physical, emotional, or sexual abuse. Maybe you grew up in a dysfunctional family where your dad and mom suffered with alcoholism or drug addiction. Or maybe you have grown up with a single parent and feel a deep void, missing your mom or dad. For others, you may have experienced something else in life that causes you to really question God. If God is so loving, why did He put me in so much pain? Why does He allow this to happen in my life? How can I love a God who constantly allows trouble in my life?

Unfortunately, traumatic experiences can manifest in negative thought patterns and behaviors. Some of you might feel as though you're not valuable, capable, or gifted. Or you might struggle finding what you really enjoy because you grew up living most of your life in survival mode. You're hustling to pay the bills. Thinking about your identity and calling seems too much of a luxury. Or you might be driven to prove that you are a somebody. Some of you might distrust God and blame Him for allowing these difficult situations in your life.

In a recent study, Barna Group asked adults in the United States how many factors influenced their personal identity. The number one factor cited for influencing self-identity is family. Just because you had to suffer traumatic experiences in your family doesn't mean you can't change. There is hope.

You are invited to be part of God's family, but there is one condition. You must accept Jesus Christ as your Savior and Redeemer. Every human being was created by God, but not everyone becomes His child. The only way to enter into His family is by being born again. When you die to yourself and are born again, God adopts you as His son or daughter. Then we become His children, other believers become our brothers and sisters, and the church becomes our spiritual family. We don't deserve to be His children, but He has chosen us, loved us, and given His only son Jesus Christ to die for our sins so that we might become His.

My dad was a mover and a shaker in the business world. He recently retired as the president of Korea's largest electronics company. The voices that told me I wasn't good enough in comparison to him—combined with societal pressures and my parents' expectations—ultimately controlled me. Slowly, I began to define myself by what those voices said. As a result, I developed a serious inferiority complex. At my core, I felt completely inadequate, ill-equipped, and thoroughly lost. I became overly self-conscious and self-critical.

The story is told of a nurse who spent several years caring for patients in the last twelve weeks of their lives. As she walked with her patients through the last moments of their lives, she observed how many of her patients gained "phenomenal clarity of vision" as they approached death. When the patients were questioned about any regrets they had or anything they would do differently, the top regret was not having the courage to live a life for themselves—not the life others expected of them.[3] We are living under enormous pressure to be people we were not meant to be. But we must seek identity in God to rid ourselves of this pressure.

Everyone is somewhat a product of their upbringing: schooling, culture, parental expectations, or early life experiences. These factors often become driving forces, and they also influence a set of "oughts and shoulds" about our lives. For example, if you happen to be an Asian American twentysomething working in New York City, you feel the pull of all sorts of "oughts and shoulds" that are layered into your life. Some driving forces might come from the values of your first-generation Asian parents. Others might come from your unique upbringing in an inner-city environment. Understanding which environmental factors may influence you will help you differentiate which voices are coming from the world and which are coming from God.

What voices are you listening to now? In my twenties, God started to help me differentiate which ideas and thoughts were from Him or the world.

LET'S SEE YOUR ID

If you were asked to identify yourself, you would show some form of ID. This might be your driver's license, an employee badge, a credit card, or your passport. To gain access to buildings at my former workplace, I used two IDs: my driver's license and my employee badge.

We live in a culture where people are fearful of identity theft. My credit card and personal information have been stolen a few times, and it's a panicky situation. When someone uses your login ID, password, or credit card numbers, they can take away everything you have.

Your identity is the cornerstone of defining your purpose in life. The problem is that many of what we often identify ourselves with can be lost, whether that is our job, our family, our house, or our car. It happens when your parents or spouses pass away, or when you leave a job that you've worked hard at for so many years. We can feel as if we have lost everything when we base our identity in things that prove to be temporary.

Like the ID we carry to show our physical identity, we also have spiritual identities that point us to the Creator. It all starts with the Bible, the Word of God, which sheds light on our spiritual DNA. What you anchor your identity to will either make or break your life.

FINDING YOUR IDENTITY IN CHRIST

As a Millennial, I see so many of us living in spiritual high school. Many of you might be stuck in a juvenile faith. The reason why there's such a struggle is because we don't know who we are. This lack of awareness of who we are makes our faith legalistic.

During my struggle to discover my identity, I came across the following poignant words by C. S. Lewis: "The more we get what we now call 'ourselves' out of the way and let Him take us over, the more truly ourselves we become…It is when I turn to Christ, when I give myself up to His personality, that I first begin to have a real personality of my own…Sameness is to be found most among the most 'natural' men, not among those who surrender to Christ."[4]

We can only find our real selves when we define ourselves in light of our Caller. I didn't find my true self by seeking more of me; I found my true self by seeking God.

I discovered this insight in an unusual verse from Scripture.

In Psalm 17:8 (NIV), David says to God, "Keep me as the apple of your eye." Most of us heard of "apple of one's eye." It's a familiar line, a cliché even, but I became curious to learn the story behind this idiom. The "apple" of my eye refers to the pupil of my eye. Since the apple was one of the most common circular-shaped objects around, the pupil was referred to as the apple. The more literal translation of the Hebrew actually means "little man of my eye"—even more confusing. But imagine looking into someone's eye right now. If you stand very close and look long enough, you notice your reflection.

When you have an intimate relationship with God and look at Him long enough, you begin to see an accurate reflection of yourself, no more distorted reflections of what the world says you should be. You get to see your real self. This insight led me on a journey of radical reorientation based on who the Bible told me I was.

KNOW WHOSE YOU ARE

The only way you can fight against external voices and pressures is to develop a robust sense of confidence and satisfaction about who you are. But it's so hard to know who you are if you don't know *whose* you are.

Every day I read a chapter of the Book of Proverbs corresponding with the date of the month. On March 22, 2015, I read Proverbs 22. Verse 1 says, "A good name is rather to be chosen than great riches, and loving favor rather than silver and gold."

I have wondered, what's in a name? Over the last ten years, I've had the opportunity to travel to different countries and speak at various conferences and organizations. Before I leave for one of these engagements, my mom has always reminded me, "Remember who you are." As the eldest child, I have a paramount responsibility to lead the family and not to tarnish the family name. My Korean name is Jaesang, which translates into prime minister. In essence, my mom was reminding me to fully represent my name every time and place.

Here's the thing: God says that when we personally invite Jesus Christ into our lives as Lord and Savior, we enter into his family as children. John 1:12 (NIV) says, "Yet to all who did receive him, to those who believed in his name, he gave the right to become children of God." And 2 Chronicles 7:14 (NIV) says, "My people, who are called by my name."

Just as Abram became Abraham, Jacob became Israel, and Simon was replaced by Peter, I have been given a new name. Like a bride who takes on the name of the groom and drops her maiden name, I have been given a new name. My new name carries a holy reputation that is not to be defiled. I would hate to tarnish the name of Jesus Christ.

Leonard Sweet said, "Your life is not your own: it belongs to God. To be yourself is to be and do what God wants you to be and do, knowing that God created you for a mission and knows you and your mission better than you do."[5]

You belong to Christ—as Christ's possession. Imagine that. You were bought at a hefty price: the blood of Jesus Christ. Jesus Christ, the God incarnate, who was sinless, died for you, an utterly sinful being. Only at the cross of crucifixion can we be born again to live our lives under the lens of Jesus. That is us. Our life is in the hands of the Lord. God is in control of your life.

Until you settle your identity in Christ, you will be vulnerable to insecurity and the pressure of competing voices. You cannot pursue your calling and serve like Jesus until you settle this issue. Realize that because you belong to Him, you are extremely valuable.

When you are in Christ, you're not an ordinary person. You're the child of the living God. You're not just a sinner; you're a new creation in Jesus. You're one of God's chosen people, a joint heir with Jesus Christ. So, have you made your pledge of allegiance to our Creator?

FORGIVEN AND SAVED BY GRACE

When I talk to some friends in my generation, I notice how much shame has taken root in their lives. They're not living up to their potential and feel like their lives are falling apart. Their sense of shame often comes from wounds and mistakes that seem irreversible. When you are in Christ, He has forgiven you. Whatever crap you have gone through, let it go. God, the Creator and the Author of your life, has forgiven you. The apostle Paul wrote in Colossians, "When you were dead in your sins and in the uncircumcision of your sinful nature, God made you alive with Christ. He forgave us all our sins, having canceled the charge of our legal indebtedness, which stood against us and condemned us; he has taken it away, nailing it to the cross" (Col. 2:13–14 NIV).

Ravi Zacharias shares a powerful story on forgiveness. He shares a poem written by an elementary teacher. I came across a powerful story listening to Ravi Zacharias's sermon on forgiveness. Here's a poem written by an elementary teacher:

He came to my desk with a quivering lip,
the lesson was done.
"Have you a new sheet for me, dear teacher?
I've spoiled this one."
I took his sheet, all soiled and blotted

and gave him a new one all unspotted.
And into his tired heart I cried,
"Do better now, my child."
I went came to the throne with a trembling heart;
the day was done.
"Have you a new day for me, dear Master?
I've spoiled this one."
He took my day, all soiled and blotted
and gave me a new one all unspotted.
And into my tired heart he cried,
"Do better now, my child."[6]

Like the child, you might feel like your life is tainted, adulterated, and void of happiness. But when you ask for forgiveness of your sins, God erases everything. You are no longer subjected to live under the yoke of the world. You are forgiven by grace.

YOU ARE GOD'S MASTERPIECE

Not only do we join God as a member of His family, God says we are His workmanship. In other words, we are His masterpiece. It says in Ephesians, "For we are his workmanship, created in Christ Jesus for good works, which God prepared beforehand, that we should walk in them."

The word *workmanship* means that we are handcrafted by God. In Greek, workmanship is *poeima*, which means "work of art." This is where we get our English words *poem* and *poetry*. In essence, we are God's poem in motion. How beautiful is that!

The story is told of Rick Warren's visit to a prison, where he spoke to approximately five thousand inmates. Nobody was paying attention to him. He was standing on an even ground with no stage, just a microphone that could be heard throughout the entire prison. He pulled out a fifty-dollar bill, held it up, and said, "How many of you would like this fifty-dollar bill?" Five thousand hands went up. He had everybody's attention. Then he crumpled it in his hands, tore it a bit, and said, "How many of you would still like this fifty-dollar bill?" Five thousand hands went up. Then he spat on the fifty-dollar bill, threw it on the ground, stomped it into the dirt, held it up, and said, "How many of you would like it now?" Five thousand hands went up.

Then Rick Warren said, "Now for many of you, this is what your father did to you. You've been mistreated. You are abused. You are misused. You were told that you wouldn't amount to anything. You've done a lot of dumb things too. You sinned. You've done some crimes, and you're paying for them. You've been beaten. You've been torn. You've been dirty, but you have not lost one cent of your value to God."[7]

A lot of us have done stupid things at one point or another. We carry this burden of shame in our lives. We often turn to work and professionalism to hide our insecurities. Let me tell you: Whatever wrong you have done, God loves you. He loves you for who you are, not what you have done. The value of who you are has never changed.

Remember the parable of the shepherd? God immediately goes after the one lost sheep. That's how much He loves you. His love knows no bounds. God's love is so great that it will descend to any depth and go to any length to save you. The greatest testament of love is the cross of Jesus Christ. He sent His only son to die for us, sinners who do not deserve His love. But that's how much He loves you.

Remember the words of the psalmist: "Where can I go from Your Spirit? Or where can I flee from Your presence? If I ascend into heaven, You are there; if I make my bed in Sheol, behold, You are there. If I take the wings of the dawn, and dwell in the remotest part of the sea, even there Your hand will lead me, and Your right hand will lay hold of me" (Ps. 139:7–10 NASB).

You're not an accident. You weren't mass-produced and stamped from an assembly line. Rather, you were intentionally designed, specially gifted, and lovingly positioned on the earth by the Creator and Author of life. When you see your identity with the lens of how your Creator sees you, you will find a deep, profound fulfillment.

EXERCISE: CHANGING YOUR CRITICAL SELF-TALK

Everyone has inner dialogue. How we talk to ourselves greatly impacts how we feel. The truth is that we act the way we feel, we feel the way we think, and we think the way we believe.

If you feel hopeless or depressed, the reason may come from wrong beliefs about yourself as a result of negative self-talk.

According to behavioral psychologists, as much as 77 percent of self-talk is negative or works against you. And it takes as many as twenty positive statements about yourself to counteract one negative statement about yourself.[8] Often, we entertain negative thoughts because of what others have said to us. We've been called ugly, stupid, and moronic. Satan is a master at this. He tries to deceive your mind and emotions to make you think that you're not worthy, that you're not loved, and that you're not going to measure up to the expectations of the world.

Here are two tips on how to silence your inner critic:

1. Journal your thoughts.

Whenever you're feeling bad about something, write down what you just said to yourself. Try to be as honest and accurate as possible. What words do you actually use when you're self-critical?

For instance, when you go on a self-loathing binge, does your self-talk sound something like "you're disgusting" or "you make me sick"? Take note of phrases like "I should" or "I have to." For instance, "I am frustrated because I should be better than this. I shouldn't be experiencing depression at all."

2. Replace negative self-talk with Scripture.

God's Word affirms our value and worth in Jesus Christ. The fact is, you and I were created for a divine purpose, and God loves us unconditionally. By memorizing and meditating on Scripture, you can renew your pattern of thinking based on what God says rather than what man has said. Practice speaking the following Scriptures to yourself out loud until it becomes your habit to speak truthful words about yourself instead of the lies with which Satan often infests our minds.

- I am God's child. (John 1:12)

- I am a branch of Jesus Christ, the True Vine, and a channel of His life. (John 15:5)

- As a disciple, I am a friend of Jesus Christ. (John 15:15)

- I have been chosen to bear fruit. (John 15:6)

- I am free from condemnation. (Rom. 8:1–2)

- I am assured that God works for my good in all circumstances. (Rom. 8:28)

- I am free from any condemnation brought against me, and I cannot be separated from the love of God. (Rom. 8:31–39)

- I am united with the Lord, and I am one with Him in spirit. (1 Cor. 6:17)

- I am God's temple. (I Cor. 3:16)

- I have been bought with a price, and I belong to God. (1 Cor. 6:19–20)

- I am a member of Christ's body. (1 Cor. 12:27)

- I have been established, anointed, and sealed by God. (2 Cor. 1:21–22)

- I have been chosen by God and adopted as His child. (Eph. 2:6)

- I am God's workmanship. (Eph. 2:10)

- I am confident that God will complete the good work He started in me. (Phil. 1:6)

- I can do all things through Christ, who strengthens me. (Phil. 4:13)

- I have been redeemed and forgiven of all my sins. (Col. 1:13–14)

- I have not been given a spirit of fear but of power, love, and a sound mind. (2 Tim. 1:7)

I was born a Korean and raised in Korea, the US, and Canada. Now I am a resident of the United States. But, at the end of the day, I am a citizen of heaven, a child of God, His workmanship, and His sheep. Jesus is our Good Shepherd. He calls us to be defined by Him, not by the standards of the world or our own critical self-talk. Only when we know *whose* we are can we discover *who* we are. Only when we discover who we are can we discover our divine assignment. It's the prerequisite of living in our sweet spot.

QUESTIONS FOR REFLECTION AND DISCUSSION

1. What self-spoken statements and whose voices have defined your identity thus far?

2. How have the competing voices prevented you from finding your identity in Christ?

3. What is one step you can take to move toward finding your true identity?

PART III

CALLING 101

CHAPTER 5

What Is Your Calling?

"Deep in our hearts, we all want to find and fulfill a purpose bigger than ourselves. Only such a larger purpose can inspire us to heights we know we could never reach on our own. For each of us the real purpose is personal and passionate: to know what we are here to do, and why."

—*Os Guinness*

What does it mean to be called? A spectrum of examples comes to mind for how the word *calling* is used. You might hear a college student say he got calls from NYU, Emory, and Boston College. But he says he found *his* calling at Baylor. This may cause you to wonder what exactly calls us toward something. Or, in an ad for a seminary, if a student says, "I wanted to be a CEO, but God called me to something greater. I sensed God was calling me to be in full-time ministry," it may raise the question of whether a sacred calling is more valuable than a secular calling. Or, a caption in an ad for a mobile phone with vibration reads, "I can feel when somebody is calling me. It's not supernatural; it's technological." But how do we know when we receive God's call in a noisy world?

Os Guinness shares a helpful definition of calling. He says

calling is "the truth that God calls us to himself so decisively that everything we are...do...and have is invested with a special devotion, dynamism, and direction lived out as a response to his summons and service."[1]

When you actively seek to live your life according to God's call, he reveals that call to you. You can feel it, and you know that you have begun to live in your sweet spot.

I know that I've found my call because now I wake up every morning with an incredible sense of anticipation and joy. The biggest change in how I feel was what I chose as my source of motivation. Before, I was driven. I was preoccupied with material symbols of achievement. I was addicted in the uncontrolled pursuit of expansion. Now, I am called. I live and work with an unwavering sense of purpose. I embrace littleness, hiddenness, and powerlessness. I am liberated from my walls of self-preservation. God is directing my path.

Here are some definitions that helped expand my understanding of calling.

- *"God's personal invitation for me to work on His agenda using the talents I've been given in ways that are eternally significant."*—Brad Lomenick, former president of Catalyst Conference
- *"A God-given purpose to use one's time, energy, and abilities to serve God in the world."*—Gerald Lawson Sittser, professor and chair of theology at Whitworth University
- *"The work that [a person] is called to do in this world, the thing that he is summoned to spend his life doing...We can speak of a man choosing his vocation, but perhaps it is at least as accurate to speak of a vocation's choosing the man, of a call being given and a man's hearing it, or not hearing it."*—Parker

Palmer, founder and senior partner of the Center for Courage and Renewal

- *"God's shaping of your burden and beckoning you to your service to him in the place and pursuit of his choosing."*—Ravi Zacharias, Christian apologist

WHO IS CALLING?

You now know that you cannot fully realize your calling until you discover the caller. That may be a difficult concept for some because it means that calling does not start and end with ourselves. Rather, calling denotes that someone else is calling.

Before we are called to something, we are called to Someone. Before we are called to do, we are called to be. The idea that we are the captain of our souls, the designer who can choose our destiny, is false.

I like what Os Guinness shares in *The Call*: "If there is no Caller, there are no callings—only work." Calling means someone has called you. Without knowing the Caller, how do we know whether the call is legitimate? Only when we know the character and identity behind the Caller can our calling carry deeper significance. I believe only when we get to know the Creator behind the creation can we discover what brings joy to the Creator.

This raises the question, who is our Creator? What can we know about Him? The Bible says God created us. He is the Author of our life. We need to allow God to be in complete control of our lives.

The reason why our lives carry eternal significance is because there is a Caller.

Tim Keller said:

Everyone will be forgotten, nothing we do will make any difference, and all good endeavors, even the best, will come to naught. Unless there is God. If the God of the Bible exists, and there is a True Reality beneath and behind this one, and this life is not the only life, then every good endeavor, even the simplest ones, pursued in response to God's calling, can matter forever.[2]

Rebekah Lyons also shares profound perspective about how we ought to respond to God's call:

We have to excavate the layers that are covering the simplicity of calling. We're the ones who complicated it by trying to meet expectations or be enough so that we can have the approval of man. The point of calling is it really strips away what man thinks is important and it comes back to this purity of heart that says, "No this is actually something assigned by God. And I'm supposed to either say yes to that or no and ignore it."[3]

So what's your choice? Are you going to respond to His call?

THE DIFFERENCE BETWEEN CALLING, JOB, AND CAREER

Calling is such a complicated word. To some, it's a way to affirm that people are living a purpose-driven life. For others, it may feel like a prison. It binds them to something that they didn't get to choose. For others, calling is a luxury. It's for the privileged—while you may be hustling to make ends meet.

People hear the word *calling* and they interpret it in so many different ways.

The world is flooded with books that promise to help you find your calling. I've devoured many books in the self-help section of bookstores that give their advice on how to live out your life's purpose. I've tried and implemented all their strategies and have still felt a gnawing emptiness.

You may have felt this growing sense of emptiness and feeling of helplessness. More and more people seem to be finding their calling, and you feel like you're missing out, not knowing exactly what it is. You may have heard people older than you saying, "Look at all the gifts you have. Why aren't you using them?"

In order to feel good about ourselves, we deceive ourselves, believing that career is tantamount to calling. One astute observer wrote, "Students had become careerists" whose "life decisions were determined not out of a sense of vocation, but in terms of career."[4]

So many bright, aspiring young professionals choose their jobs based on salary expectations. But what if I told you that calling isn't synonymous to career or job? What if calling transcends a career in the same way an athlete transcends the sport he or she plays?

Marianne Williamson put it perfectly: "Jobs come and go, but a calling is something you were given the moment you were born. You can lose a job, but you can't lose your calling."[5] When you have a career, you build a resume. When you have a calling, you coauthor your life story with God.

Calling often uses a career, though calling cannot be reduced simply to a career. Your calling is much more than a career or job. It's like an umbrella that covers every aspect of your life, which your job and career fits under. You might be called to be a leader, but that doesn't mean you necessarily must have a leadership title in your job.

PRIMARY CALLING

First and foremost, we are called to be a follower of Jesus Christ. This primary calling is a calling "to be." It is a call to Someone, not a call to do something. We are called by the ultimate Caller, God Himself, who desires to be in communion with us. He calls us into a personal relationship with Him. Os Guinness describes primary calling this way: "Our primary calling as followers of Christ is by Him, to Him, and for Him."[6]

God desires fellowship with us. God is far more interested in who you are than what you do. No matter how many accolades and pedigrees we showcase to God He is never impressed. Rather, He is impressed more by our character and our willingness to grow into the likeness of Christ.

However, because of sin we were separated from God by sin. We became like an electric lamp whose cord has been cut exactly in half and has lost its connection to the power source. We have all have sinned and "fallen short" of God's standard (Rom. 3:23). We need his help to "repair" our brokenness, restore the power connection, and make us whole again.

The Bible tells us that we are called to God primarily in four ways. We are primarily called to faith in Christ (Rom. 8:28–30; 1 Cor. 1:9; 2 Thess. 2:10–12), into the kingdom of God (1 Thess. 2:10–12), to eternal life (1 Tim. 6:12; Heb. 9:15), and to holy living (1 Cor. 1:2; 1 Pet. 1:15). Your primary calling is to put your relationship with God at the forefront of your life.

Surely your goodness and love will follow me all the days of my life, and I will dwell in the house of the LORD forever.

SECONDARY CALLING

Secondary calling is a calling "to do." Calling, in this sense, means being called as a student, an accountant, a mother, an artist, etc. Secondary calling is a specific call to action that reflects the uniqueness God endowed us with.

While everyone's primary calling is the same—that is, to be in God's presence as a follower of Jesus Christ—our secondary calling is distinct for each person.

This type of calling includes both our career plans and the daily ordinary tasks that come as part of our everyday life.

Hugh Whelchel, the founder of Institute for Faith, Work and Economics, describes four aspects of secondary callings that will help us better live our lives.[7]

First, one of the most defining and natural secondary callings is a call to our human family. You are born into the family and you grow up playing the role of a brother, sister, son, daughter, father, or mother at some point in your life. God established marriage first in the Garden of Eden and commanded us to be fruitful and multiply. Our call in our human family is a way to carry on God's cultural mandate.

Second, you are called to the church. The church is the body of Christ where all members possess and use their spiritual gifts to strengthen the body of Christ. The diversity of gifts further strengthens the church "until we all reach unity in the faith and in the knowledge of the Son of God and become mature, attaining to the whole measure of the fullness of Christ" (Eph. 4:13 NIV).

Third, we are called to our neighbors. C. S. Lewis said, "Next to the Blessed Sacrament itself, your neighbor is the holiest object presented to your senses."[8] Your neighbors are the community outside the church and family. This could be your physical neighbors or acquaintances you've met at work or school.

Last, we are called vocationally. This is the most commonly understood aspect of secondary calling. In essence, work fits into this aspect of calling. Like Dorothy Sayers wrote, work is "not, primarily as a thing one does to live, but the thing one lives to do... [Work] is, or it should be, the full expression of the worker's gifts, the thing in which he finds spiritual, mental, and bodily satisfaction, and the medium in which he offers himself to God."[9]

We need to balance the primary and secondary calling in order to avoid distortions. Like Peter, we face two significant callings. Primarily, we are called to salvation; secondarily, we are called to respond to a specific direction in terms of work. For Peter, this reflected his call to be an apostle, "a fisher of men." We too are called to an area of work or vocation that expresses who God has uniquely created us to be. It's important that we understand our secondary calling in light of our primary calling.

Secondary calling matters only in light of our primary calling. Many seek to discover their secondary calling while they ignore their primary calling. This results in a sense of incompleteness.

MULTIPLE CALLINGS

We should learn to think of calling in the plural. In fact, most of us have multiple callings. Our secondary callings go beyond being our occupations. But I've seen many of my type-A friends, and I myself, live for and by a career.

This is problematic because when your vocational calling takes precedence over other callings in your life, you experience an unnerving disequilibrium. If you are currently going to school, you are called as a student. If you are married, you are called to be a spouse. If you have children, you are called to be a parent. You might also have various callings within your family (son, daughter, brother, sister, uncle, aunt). If you attend church, you might be called as a deacon or an elder.

Secondary callings also change over time. When you get married, you begin a new calling as a husband or wife. Or, they may be temporary. When you graduate from college, your calling as a student ends and transitions into something else. When we're younger, we tend to focus our identity so much on work, partly because not all of our secondary callings have occurred. But we need to be patient as God reveals calling to us over time.

Jeff Goins chooses to see his calling as a portfolio. "The portfolio life," as he calls it, "is when you are not just a student or a young professional, but also a son, daughter, husband, or wife."

According to Goins, the basic idea of a portfolio life is that instead of thinking of your work as a monolithic activity, what if you chose to see it as the complex group of interests, passions, and activities it is? And what if instead of identifying with a job description, you began to see the whole mass of things you do as one portfolio of activity?[10]

Life can be a messy process where we are constantly juggling the balls of various callings. It requires us to assume responsibility and stewardship of these various callings.

THE CENTERED LIFE VERSUS THE
COMPARTMENTALIZED LIFE

The challenges we face while trying to live out our multiple callings are real. How do I continue to live out my callings intentionally when it seems several of my callings seem incompatible or conflicting? You may have heard stories of successful businessmen who are well respected in their organizations and community but have failed miserably as a father and husband. It might look like your calling as a father or husband might prevent you from becoming a successful businessman. Your calling as a college student may seem to go against your responsibilities as a student leader in your church. Sadly, what often happens is that we live a fragmented life.

Therefore, we often respond to these competing demands by compartmentalizing our lives. But it is frustrating to feel like a different person at work than we are at home. Instead of feeling inauthentic and divided, we yearn for connectedness and integration.

For a long time, I lived this type of life—a highly compartmentalized life. I was one person when I was with my inner circle of friends, a completely different person in church, and yet another person at work. Living an inauthentic and divided life made me feel as if my spirit was choking. I was slowly suffocating. The growing disparity between myself at work and at home left me feeling sick. I felt like an impostor.

The world tells us that we must achieve a sense of balance in our lives. But the concept of balance is so subjective. This is a tension we must grapple with for our entire lives. The problem with trying to balance our lives without letting God lead is that it is exhausting and possibly futile. In a life where I strive for balance, I try to stay in complete control of everything—work, family, personal care, friendships, community life, and political involvement—instead of allowing God to lead.

In Jack Fortin's *The Centered Life*, he provides a refreshing alternative to the balanced life, which he calls the centered life:

> The problem with this ["balanced life"] is that it keeps us self-absorbed, and the elements of our lives rarely stay in balance. Think of what happens, for example, when you have a sick child. Your goal then is not to maintain a balance, but to take immediate care of that child. The alternative to a balanced life is a faithful life. It is a life faithful, moment by moment, to the God in whom we live and move and have our being. It is a centered life. The perfect example of the faithful life is Jesus Christ. Jesus often worked long hours despite the objections of his disciples, and at other times he withdrew from people and tended to his own needs for rest, reflection, and prayer...A life centered in the triune God gives identity and a place to stand in a chaotic and compartmentalized world. The Creator God is present in all I do. Christ is the example and provides the means for how I am to live and love in God's world. The Holy Spirit is the voice within me that guides the way I live. With God as the center of my life, I know whose I am and can begin to discover who I am.[11]

Living our lives without knowing our calling is like trying to find our way out of an Amazonian jungle without any sort of navigational tool. Only when you begin to understand the depth and significance of your calling do you get to journey toward an intentional life and have eternal impact.

EXERCISE: STEWARDING MULTIPLE CALLINGS

Calling is rarely singular, but plural. Learning how to steward your role in the multiple callings will help you build a foundation that will help you start strong and finish well.

The following is the visual tool that will identify your five areas of calling.

Identify key roles you play in each circle and what responsibility you have for each calling.

- Self:

- Family:

- Friends:

- College/work:

- Community:

QUESTIONS FOR REFLECTION AND DISCUSSION

1. How has your notion of calling been challenged by the two distinctions of calling (primary calling and secondary calling)?

2. Make a list of your various secondary callings (e.g., spouse, parent, friend, neighbor, employee, volunteer, church member). How are these roles enhanced by your primary calling, or do these roles detract from it?

CHAPTER 6

Demystifying Calling

"Every person, of every degree, state, sex, or condition without exception, must have some personal and particular calling to walk in."

—*William Perkins*

You might have struggled to discover your calling because calling is a rather profound topic. Just ask around how people view calling and you might get scores of different interpretations of it. In addition, throughout history and culture, the meaning of culture has been distorted, which has created a number of misunderstandings.

The following are the most common pitfalls of calling that might prevent you from discovering your calling in life.

PITFALL 1: SPIRITUAL CALLING IS MORE IMPORTANT THAN SECULAR CALLING.

One of my friends always used to say, "I don't feel as if I'm glorifying God at work. I'm seriously considering getting into full-time ministry." Like my friend, you might have wondered the same thing. Or you might know people who have entertained similar thoughts. This idea that spiritual calling is inherently more important than secular calling is commonly known as the sacred-secular divide. In this conversation, my friend implied that spiritual work, such as being a pastor, priest, or missionary, was full-time ministry, while secular pursuits in areas such as arts, business, media, law, politics, and social services were considered part-time ministry. Os Guinness calls this the "Catholic Distortion," because it arose in the Catholic era and is a position of the Catholic tradition.

My friend is one of the thousands of Christians who have adopted this belief, that spiritual calling is superior to secular callings. However, the Bible says that all Christians are called to full-time Christian work, doing all for the glory of God, regardless of their unique vocational calling.

The distortion originates from a Roman historian called Eusebius. He was the first to talk about the concept of the "two ways of life." He argued that God allowed the "perfect life"—sacred callings dedicated to contemplation such as priests, nuns, and monks—and "permitted life," which are lowly, secular callings dedicated to actions like farming, homemaking, and soldiering.[1]

Sadly, even today, many churches fail to teach a biblical perspective of calling. Many believers have bought into the soul-suffocating myth that their work is not as important and honoring to God compared to those whose calling is in the church. This has resulted in many Christians withdrawing from their workplace and entering ministry rather than serving as the salt and light of this world. This distortion has caused many Millennials to move over to the nonprofit sector with the hope that it would lead them to live a life of significance.

All callings are equal before God. All callings are sacred. There is no mention in the Bible that spiritual calling is superior to secular calling. All callings are spiritual. Working outside of full-time ministry does not make you a second-class Christian. Whether you're a pastor, missionary, entrepreneur, nurse, or office worker, God operates out of divine egalitarianism.

When you understand that all of culture is under God's authority and that He equips each of you to follow your unique calling, it becomes clear that all work should be considered Christian service. Christians in the secular environment are fulfilling God's call to be His stewards by developing culture. To be sure, some are called to vocational ministry as members of the clergy, but their work is no more or less sacred than the business owner or laborer who does her or his work as a calling from God. In fact, we need more gospel-infused, Jesus-adoring, Spirit-empowered Christ followers in Hollywood, government, technology, church, and education. As the apostle Paul said, "So whether you eat or drink or whatever you do, do it all for the glory of God" (1 Cor. 10:31 NIV).

The Coram Deo Life

The biblical idea of calling can be found in this Latin term *coram Deo*. To live *coram Deo* means "to live one's entire life in the presence of, or before the face of, God . . . under the authority of God, to the glory of God."[2]

In other words, whatever we do on this earth can never be acted outside of the penetrating gaze of God. God is omnipotent and omniscient. When we recognize His sovereignty in our lives, our "being" and "doing" is a vehicle to offer ourselves as a living sacrifice, in response to the gratitude and adoration of His love and sovereignty.

To live a *coram Deo* life is to live a whole life where everything we do is under a unifying, coherent life. This means that if you fulfill your calling as a teacher, attorney, homemaker, then you are acting every bit as religiously as a soul-winning missionary who fulfills his vocation. You cannot compartmentalize your calling to a sacred or secular life. The big idea is that every aspect of life is religious. To divide life between sacred and secular is itself a sacrilege.

William Wilberforce almost missed his calling. When he came to Christ at age twenty-five, he was one of the youngest members of parliament. In search of God's will for his life, Wilberforce visited John Newton, a former slave trader–turned–pastor. The young statesman told Newton that God was more interested in religion than politics. Wilberforce shared his plan to leave his calling as an MP to enter into vocational ministry. Newton disagreed about what was eternally significant and suggested that God might have a plan for him in parliament.

Thankfully, Wilberforce listened. Without his efforts on abolition of slavery, we would live in a completely different world. On October 28, 1787, Wilberforce wrote in his journal, "God Almighty has set before me two great objects, the suppression of the Slave Trade and the reformation of Manners [moral values]."[3] The young parliamentarian had discovered the "good works God had prepared in advance" for him—but works that would cost the British economy dearly.

Using his God-given abilities, Wilberforce turned his country from atrocious evil and gave his countrymen the moral backbone to endure the financial recession brought on by emancipation. And as the British economy suffered, God's kingdom grew. A revival that had begun in the lower classes in the 1700s erupted into the middle and upper classes in the 1800s, and altered Britain's moral compass. Lincoln's antislavery movement was profoundly inspired by the example of Wilberforce.

There is not a dichotomy between holy and unholy vocations. God never said that those working in the church world were superior to those in the secular field. Don't let the myth of secular-sacred divide inhibit you from living out your calling. In fact, your work matters to God. If you are in a secular career that doesn't violate Scripture, your calling matters. Now, the more important question is how are you living out your calling in the field you're called to?

PITFALL 2: YOUR CALLING SHOULD CENTER ON YOUR IDEAL CAREER.

Today, we live in a work-centric generation. Think back to the last time you met a person for the first time. The most commonly asked question—"What do you do?"—tells you that we live in a generation in which our identity is intimately tied with how we spend our nine-to-five at our job.

In response to the Catholic Distortion, the Protestant Reformation sparked a newfound interest in work as a central aspect of our calling. The reformation led to an extreme and unbalanced understanding of calling as simply "employment" and "job." The Protestant Distortion inadvertently stripped the word *calling* of its religious significance altogether.

Calling in this sense becomes an idol, the society's god. An idol is anything that puts something above God and captures the wonder of your heart and imagination more than God.

When you worship your work, you end up having a call without the Caller. The Caller becomes replaced by the caller with a lowercase *c*. In other words, you become the caller of your own self. Your work no longer serves God, but rather becomes self-serving. Work becomes all about advancing your own goals and needs. You find yourself living for the sake of climbing the ladder. Life becomes all about winning.

Os Guinness said it best in his book *The Call*:

> Do we enjoy our work, love our work, virtually worship our work so that our devotion to Jesus is off center? Do we put our emphasis on service, usefulness or being productive in working for God—at his expense? Do we strive to prove our own significance? To make a difference in the world? To carve our names in marble on the mountains of time? The call of God blocks the path of all such deeply human tendencies. We are not primarily called to do something or go somewhere; we are called to someone. We are not called to special work but to God. The key to answering the call is to be devoted to no one and to nothing above God himself.[4]

The Protestant Distortion states that hard work is your calling. Period. However, neither work nor career can be fully satisfying without a deeper sense of calling—but calling itself is empty and indistinguishable from work unless there is Someone who calls. God normally calls us along our line of giftedness, but the purpose of giftedness is stewardship and service, not selfishness. This secular distortion of calling results in careerism where our goal becomes achieving financial success, security, access to power, and privilege.

A sense of calling should precede a choice of job and career. Instead of "You are what you do," calling says, "Do what you are."

PITFALL 3: GOD ONLY CALLS THE QUALIFIED.

When I turned twenty-five, I felt like God was working on something big in my life. He was leading me to the path less traveled. He led me to the right books and mentors who have helped reorient my vision of success in life. For the next several years, I began applying the concepts I'm sharing in this book. He was shaping me, molding me to become the person I am today.

The more I felt God was transforming my life, the more I felt a growing urge to share this message with the greater public. The desire to write a book became greater every day. I felt this was a divine assignment from God. However, I felt thoroughly inadequate and unqualified to write such a book. After all, who I am to write a book on a profound topic like calling? I'm only in my mid-twenties. I don't have an English literature background or awards for writing. I felt thoroughly ill-equipped to write.

One day, I read the story of Moses in the Bible. When Moses encountered God in the burning bush, his life had been in a forty-year free fall. He was a social elite in Egypt, but one angry outburst decimated his entire career, sending him into the wilderness for the next forty years. In the wilderness, his main role was to tend the sheep of his father-in-law. Then at age eighty came the unmistakable call from God: "I will send you to Pharaoh that you may bring My people, the children of Israel, out of Egypt" (Ex. 3:10 NKJV).

Moses was doubtful he was suited to do the job. He felt inadequate. He wasn't eloquent, and he had lost all his confidence. But he answered the call anyway.

In many ways, I could relate to Moses. Most people I met in college were incredulous when I disclosed my entire life story. They always viewed me as the quintessential driven, ambitious, type-A individual who always wanted to "change the world." Many of them assume that my life was devoid of struggle and adversity and that I lived an obstacle-free life. But those who have been closest cannot help but marvel at the dramatic changes they've witnessed in my life. At the age of nine, I moved from America to Korea. My parents put me in a Korean public school despite that I could speak no Korean. Every day was a struggle. Coupled with my diagnosis of ADHD, I not only struggled to build interpersonal relationships with classmates, but I also floundered to survive in the hypercompetitive educational culture. Every day felt like swimming in a sea of sharks. I always had to stay vigilant and alert lest I be destroyed by the pressures of the world.

One day at school, my teacher asked me to stand up and read an article in Korean in front of the entire class. I flustered and choked. All my friends started to laugh at me. They made terrible jokes at my mispronunciation and called me derogatory names. I felt completely helpless. This traumatic experience resulted in a public speaking phobia that plagued me for the next ten years of my life. I became extremely self-conscious and developed low self-esteem.

Though I have overcome much of this traumatic memory over the last decade, I still struggle from time to time. Most surprisingly, I would never have imagined God would use my very weakness and inadequacy in pursuing my calling. Today, as a leadership development consultant, I work with leaders and teams, and most of my work is public speaking. Though I have felt utterly incompetent and unqualified, God was telling me, "Paul, I got this. I have things in control. You just have to show up. I'll do the rest."

I recall someone saying, "God doesn't call the qualified. God qualifies the called." I love what D. L. Moody, evangelist and Christian educator, says: "Moses spent forty years thinking he was a somebody; forty years learning he was a nobody; and forty years discovering what God can do with a nobody."[5]

What if God could also use a nobody like me despite my limitations and lack of abilities? I began to trust in God's plan.

Madeleine L'Engle once said: "In a very real sense not one of us is qualified, but it seems that God continually chooses the most unqualified to do his work, to bear his glory. If we are qualified, we tend to think that we have done the job ourselves. If we are forced to accept our evident lack of qualification, there's no danger that we will confuse God's work with our own or God's glory with our own."[6]

When God calls the qualified, He wants us to die to ourselves because the impossible is only made possible through God. For me, this knowledge required me to muster the courage to take a leap of faith in my ultimate Caller.

Throughout the ages, God has used men and women who have all had imperfections, defects, foibles, and failures. Isaac was a daydreamer, Jacob was a cheater, Peter had a temper and denied Christ three times, David had an affair and tried to cover it up with murder, Noah got drunk. Gideon was insecure, Miriam was a gossiper, Martha was a worrier, Thomas was a doubter, Sarah was impatient, Elijah was moody, and Moses stuttered. The truth is that God has a consistent track record of handpicking those from the pit instead of the pedestal.

PITFALL 4: PURSUING CALLING IS A LUXURY
ONLY FOR THE UPPER-MIDDLE CLASS.

For many twentysomethings, the notion of calling is depressing. They see their current reality and then look at their calling. The gap seems vastly wide. For many, living out one's calling seems like a luxury, an impossibility for the masses—something only reserved for the privileged in the upper echelons of society. For a lot of twentysomethings, especially in developing countries, their entire focus is simply survival and making their ends meet.

An underlying assumption behind this notion is that living out your calling is always extraordinary. That is, calling is often what you expect in a fairy tale—a paradise where you experience nothing but joy and pleasure. A life where you get to leave a mark and create a lasting legacy. It's a world where you actually live up to your Facebook profile. No challenges. No pain and struggles.

What if I told you that most of your calling encompasses the ordinary? The truth is, most of life happens in the ordinary. This reality is in such contrast to the clarion call of this age: that our calling must be extraordinary. Let's face it. I never met anyone who wants to be the ordinary person who goes to an ordinary school, has an ordinary job, and hangs out with ordinary friends. In the name of "changing the world," we have actually missed out on everyday opportunities that God has placed before us to glorify Him and to serve others.

Case in point. Consider the life of the apostle Paul. The core of his calling was to become an apostle to the Gentiles. But, did you ever wonder how he funded himself to carry this out? He started making tents. In fact, tent making became his day job. This became part of his calling but not the centerpiece. Tent making became the vehicle that enabled him to focus on his core calling to be the apostle to the Gentiles.

Sure, you might call this not ideal, but remember that even though part of what you do to fulfill your purpose may not seem extraordinary, it is still important to your calling. When you view this part of your life as inferior, you are doing a disservice to God's overarching purpose and plan for you. Remember there are times when God doesn't call you to slay dragons. Rather, He is calling you to be an ordinary person who lives for an extraordinary God. So do you know who's calling you? Are you ready to answer? Are you ready to accept your call?

EXERCISE: A LEAP OF FAITH

Do you experience fear or perceive weakness in an area of life that you sense you must overcome in order to achieve God's ultimate purpose for you?

Consider engaging in a situation that forces you to face that fear and have faith that God will see you through.

For instance, if you're afraid to speak publicly, volunteer to share testimony at church, or give a school presentation. You may be surprised at how much you grow and how receptive others will be to your brave act of vulnerability.

If you feel the desire to help in your community but aren't sure how to get involved, make an appointment to visit a homeless shelter and volunteer to serve a meal. A smile and a friendly hello as you engage with those you meet is a wonderful place to start. Let God guide you from there.

You may be surprisingly enriched by challenging yourself. And you don't have to do it alone. Go to God in prayer and ask Him to be with you as you strive to better serve your purpose in him.

QUESTIONS FOR REFLECTION AND DISCUSSION

1. Have you felt that your contribution to the world was inferior to that of those who were in full-time ministry?

2. Do you have a personal relationship with Jesus Christ? How do you view His calling for you in relation to your own sense of calling?

3. Have you ever felt you were unqualified to pursue God's calling in your life? How has this chapter impacted that view, if at all?

4. Have you ever wondered if pursuing your calling is a luxury? How did this chapter change your perspective of calling?

PART IV

VOCATIONAL SWEET SPOT

CHAPTER 7

Discerning Your Calling

"Before I can tell my life what I want to do with it, I must listen to my life telling me who I am."

—*Parker Palmer*

Discovering God's call in your life requires you to enter a time of discernment. *Discern* is defined as "to separate, to sort out, to sift through." Discerning your calling is then a period of sifting and sorting. It is when you allow yourself to be open to God's will, letting Him guide your life more than trusting your own reasoning.

There is no one-size-fits-all formula for discerning your calling. We read how-to articles like "20 Ways to Find Your Calling" and "15 Life Hacks for Pursuing Your Calling in Life" as if they will give us the definitive list of accelerating our discovery of calling. We now know, however, that it doesn't work that way.

Much of my life I was looking for God's direct, unmistakable call. I was waiting for the "burning bush" moment that would instantly provide a new direction for my life—like when God called Noah to build the ark. Or when God called Saul (Paul) to leadership through a blinding light on the road to Damascus. Or when God called Abram and Sarah to undertake amazing journeys. I was looking for an overwhelming, dramatic experience.

But calling in this sense rarely happens in the twenty-first century. Even in the Bible, it happened to no more than a hundred people.

Most of us will not experience the burning bush call. Finding your calling is more like being on a lifelong scavenger hunt. You find important clues and advice along the way as you reflect upon your life experiences and those who guide you along the way. The key is becoming more attentive to the signs that provide hints, signposts, and a sense of direction.

THREE WAYS TO DISCERN YOUR CALLING

1. Prayerful Listening

Rather than seeking miraculous signs and answers, we need to develop a posture of attentiveness, listening to who we are and where we are. Finding your calling is more like listening for a whisper rather than a thunderous clap. Listening to your calling requires a certain amount of discipline and regularly seeking deeper intimacy with God.

In his book *Let Your Life Speak*, Parker Palmer said:

> [Calling]...comes from listening. I must listen to my life and try to understand what it is truly about—quite apart from what I would like it to be about—or my life will never represent anything real in the world, no matter how earnest my intentions. Before I can tell my life what I want to do with it, I must listen to my life telling me who I am. I must listen for the truths and values at the heart of my own identity, not the standards by which I must live—but the standards by which I cannot help but live if I am living my own life.[1]

Coming to peace with God's will in your life can only happen in a spiritual setting, that is, through an active prayer life. Only in your conversations with God can you fully sense where He may be leading you. Set aside quiet time every day and ask the Lord, "What do you want of me?" "How should I live my life today?" "In what areas do I need to grow more in your likeness?" Use Scripture in your prayer so the living Word of God will penetrate into your heart.

2. Voices of People

Calling is not discovered in isolation. The Western culture of individualism says we can do what it takes to choose our own direction. Basing a career solely on self-interest may be one of the biggest, most common sins any young person can commit, as to do so means one must implicitly withdraw from God's power.

Calling is best discerned in the context of community. The writer of Proverbs tells us, "Where there is no guidance the people fall, But in abundance of counselors there is victory" (Prov. 11:14 NASB).

As you share your deepest thoughts and questions regarding your calling in the context of Christian community, surprising insights often emerge and open our eyes and ears to what we have not seen or heard. This enlightens us and transforms us to see beyond our narrow perspective and expectations.

We must learn to listen well to those in our immediate communities. Are we listening to our family, our friends, and maybe even our foes as we consider our vocational path? There is great value in a contemplative approach to vocational discernment.

At the same time, it's easy to fall into the myth that discovering God's call from the voices of people is like a popularity contest or a public opinion poll. You need discernment to ask the right people. Our primary calling is to be a people who live in communion with our triune God. Only in community with God and others do we begin to discover our calling, occasionally like a flash of lightning, but more often haltingly.

Our calling both comes through community and is oriented toward community. We need discernment as we listen to what our community is saying.

Without the voices of others, I know I would not be where I am today in my spiritual process. God has sent me voices throughout my life—people I may have only known for a short time and others I have known for a long while. I feel so alive and filled with love when we have spiritual talks. It is their voices echoing mine that bring light and peace into my life.

Let's consider William Wilberforce again. God used three different men to call Wilberforce: the prime minister, William Pitt, who was a nonbeliever; John Newton, his spiritual mentor and creator of the popular hymn "Amazing Grace"; and John Wesley, the great Anglican minister. In the early 1790s, Wesley wrote Wilberforce to encourage the younger man to hang in there in leading the campaign against the slave trade. This was the last letter Wesley ever wrote. He was eighty-eight years old and died six days later.

Unless God has raised you up...I see not how you can go through with your glorious enterprise in opposing that execrable villainy, which is the scandal of religion, of England, and of human nature. Unless God has raised you up for this very thing, you will be worn out by the opposition of men and devils; but if God is with you, who can be against you? Oh, be not weary in well-doing. Go on, in the name of God and in the power of his might, till even American slavery, the vilest that ever saw the sun, shall banish away before it.[2]

Os Guinness thought after his conversion he should be a pastor. A ten-minute conversation with a service station attendant caused him to understand his work was outside, not inside, the church, and he became a public intellectual.

First, seek out the counsel and example of godly leaders. Your pastor, youth minister, Sunday school teacher, and spiritual mentors can all be a barometer indicating your call in life. If they raise a red flag whenever they have serious reservations about your calling, you should listen carefully.

Also, listen to your family. The Scripture says, "Hear, my son, your father's instruction, and forsake not your mother's teaching" (Prov. 1:8 ESV). However, this is tricky. Some twentysomethings come from a non-Christian family background. This is where you need discernment to know whether the advice is truly helpful. Even Christian families want the best for their children but can sometimes interpret it to gain the prestige, power, and possessions of the world. If you feel torn by a parent's advice and unsure if it's scripturally sound, I would suggest that you go confirm it with a spiritual mentor like your church pastor or church leaders. Even these spiritual mentors could lead you off track to pursue worldly desires. If you're unsure, always retreat to the Bible first and ask God for guidance.

I discovered my calling by simply asking the right questions. The questions didn't come easily, as I was struggling to muster the courage. But once the questions were asked, I found an enormous sense of relief.

Here are some questions that will help you discover God's calling:

What makes me unique?

What do you see as my spiritual gifts?

What do you see as my top three strengths?

Where do you see me maximizing my strengths?

What do you see as my weaknesses?

Where do you see my weaknesses show up?

Where and when do you see me fully alive?

Where and when do you see me lethargic?

How would you describe me in three words?

What should I stop doing?

What should I start doing?

What should I continue doing?

When have I appeared most joyful and fulfilled?

How do you see me helping build God's kingdom?

Reading missionary biographies or frontline stories of heroes of faith will inspire you as well.

3. Elements of the Sweet Spot

Discovering your calling is usually a messy process. However, in my conversations with my friends and peers in my generation, the prevailing belief is that God seems to be playing a game of hide-and-seek when it comes to calling. Many twentysomethings often believe in what I call the bull's-eye approach to calling. That is, we believe there is one perfect calling, the one thing that I'm supposed to do, one grad school, one perfect spouse, and God is playing a game of hide-and-seek. Instead, our job is to start discovering our sweet spot and act upon this discovery, which gives us the opportunity to live with greater intentionality.

A sweet spot is the intersection of four interlocking circles.

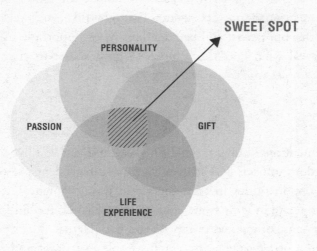

Imagine a Venn diagram. The first circle is personality, or who you are wired to be—the temperament and tendencies that make you unique. The second is gifts, or that which you are naturally gifted in—marketable skills, spiritual gifts, and strengths that some were born with and others have developed over the course of their lives. The third is passions, or what ignites a fire in your soul—those innate, divinely inspired desires that are complemented by addressing needs of the world. And the fourth is life experiences, or those doors that have both opened and closed in your life—the people, experiences, and stories that define who you are today. Where these circles interlock is your sweet spot and where you should always strive to be working closer toward if you want to live a life of significance and fulfillment.

As you seek to clarify who you are, why you are here, and where you are going, don't be surprised to see major paradigm shifts in your life. I invite you to embrace the a-ha moments. Be intentional, not accidental. It might take you weeks and months, but persist and be relentless. Most important, ask God to reveal what needs to happen to grow closer to your vocational sweet spot.

AN INTENTIONAL LIFE

An intentional life is striving for every moment you live to have kingdom impact, and stewarding your gifts, talents, resources, and opportunities to turn the world upside down. The more you operate in your sweet spot, the more you'll feel an inexplicable sense of joy and peace. As you gain clarity of *who* you are because of *whose* you are, you'll be able to reorder and realign your five spheres of influence (self, family, team, organization, community) around your calling.

QUESTIONS FOR REFLECTION AND DISCUSSION

1. What are some ways you can start to discern your calling?

2. What can you do to become more attentive to the voice of God in your life?

3. How have the voices of other people helped or hindered you from discovering your calling?

CHAPTER 8

Personality/Wiring

"Like stained glass, our different personalities reflect
God's light in many colors and patterns."

—*Rick Warren*

I grew up as a third-culture kid. I crisscrossed Korea, Canada,
the United States. The first time I came back to Korea from living in America for six years, I plugged my 110-volt hair dryer
into the 220-volt outlet. When I turned it on, it worked for
a minute until it quickly burned out. Why? Because my hair
dryer was not wired for 220 volts.

Whenever I experience burnout, meaninglessness, and emptiness in my life, I am reminded that I'm probably not wired for
the things that I'm plugged into.

When God created us in His unique image, He wired us to
be specifically who we are today. As stewards, you and I have a
responsibility to uncover our natural wiring, which helps us live
more fully in our vocational sweet spot.

Your wiring is your personality, your natural temperament.
There is a divine intention behind why you are talkative or
quiet. Why you like reading books or being outdoors working
with your hands. This is all part of how you were designed.

For the first twenty years of my life, I thought that my

personality type wasn't going to help me become successful. I envied my peers who were more vocal, outgoing, and competitive than I was, and I honestly thought they would be the ones who would make it. In fact, I grew up in a culture that cherished and rewarded extreme extroverts. When I compared myself to them, I felt I didn't measure up. I didn't think I had the Steve Jobs–like charisma to become a leader.

It took me ten years to embrace my inherent hardwiring. I was naturally more quiet, thoughtful, and easygoing. Growing up, I became enslaved by my upbringing, and the oughts and shoulds that it imposed upon my life. Whether through schooling, early life experiences, parenting, or culture, these collective experiences impacted who I am today. Only when one of my mentors helped me discover that my upbringing was taking over my nature did I realize why I felt so exhausted and stressed in my life. For so long, I was trying to become somebody I wasn't.

There are a plethora of personality assessments that can help you learn your personality and wiring. Two of my favorites are the Myers-Brigg Type Indicator (MBTI) and DiSC. My MBTI type is ENFJ and my DiSC reading is SC. Going through an in-depth overview of my personality assessment with a certified trainer helped me embrace who I am with wide-open arms.

I have found the MBTI particularly helpful. It is based on Jungian theory. Isabel Briggs Myers and Katherine C. Briggs created an instrument to identify different personality types based on someone's natural preferences. It is estimated that 2.5 million Americans take the test each year. Eighty-nine of the US Fortune 100 companies make use of MBTI for recruitment and selection purposes.

This instrument has helped me to accept who I am. No more comparisons. No more wannabes. This tool helped me realize that there is no right personality. Our individual personality is unique to us, just like our fingerprint. Learning your personality traits gives a clue to how God has placed you in the body of Christ, "For as we have many members in one body, but all the members do not have the same function, so we, being many, are one body in Christ, and individually members of one another." (Rom. 12:4–5 NKJV).

At some point, people have been abused by personality tests where they were forced to fit into a box. They were labeled with four letters, which felt rather restraining, not liberating. The point with MBTI is not to force you to conform to a type but rather to illuminate why you behave the way you do. With a certified trainer, you will better understand why you inherently act a certain way as well as how your upbringing and choices you have made influenced your current behavior.

The MBTI breaks down four pairs of dimensions that are measured on a continuum from one extreme to another. Everyone uses each pair like they use both hands. Some, however, are more comfortable using their right hand since that is how they're wired. Based on knowing what our preference is for the right hand, MBTI generates sixteen possible personality profiles resulting from the combinations of the four dimensions. Here's a brief description of the four dimensions.

First, some are extroverts and some are introverts. The key question to know where you stand is: Do you recharge your battery by being alone or by being with others? Remember, this doesn't mean that introverts can't be social or gregarious. Rather, this is about how you recharge. Extroverts are like solar panels. They are energized by being with people and enjoy being at the center of attention. Introverts on the other hand are like batteries. They often need to retire to a place where it might be reading a book, journaling, or being alone. Be honest about it. Where are you? Which rings more true to who you are?

The second dimension of MBTI is about how we process information. Sensors are more inclined to trust clear, certain, and concrete facts, while intuitives trust metaphors and think in terms of possibilities. Sensors tend to be more practical and realists. They want to know the rules. They strive toward accuracy and a methodical approach to things. Intuitives are more inclined to think in terms of possibilities. They are natural innovators. They strive toward creativity and appreciate a different approach to things.

The third dimension is thinkers and feelers. Thinkers are logical and see data first. They put business first and set objectives. They are fair but firm. Feelers, on the other hand, always strive for harmony. They see people before a task. They decide things based on what the heart tells them and focus on values.

The last dimension is about judging and perceiving. Perceivers are naturally flexible and thrive in multitasking. They thrive in spur-of-the-moment decisions. They are open to last-minute information and alternative choices. Judgers need structure and organization. They are natural planners. They seek to control their life and set concrete goals.

Knowing how others are wired helps you in school and workplaces. When a colleague of yours does something odd, you could say, "That's the silliest thing I've ever heard," or you could focus on what you know about his or her personality or temperament. When you understand each other's wiring, this will help you tailor how to communicate your message based on his or her personality.

The goal of personality assessments is not to fit you into a box. It's not about labeling you. Rather it's about knowing yourself to discover what God has in store for your life. It's an honest self-appraisal process that facilitates your discovery of natural preferences to appreciate the complexity each person brings. Obviously, one ENFJ will never be identical to another ENFJ, as upbringing and choices have influenced the person to be who he or she is today.

If you don't know your MBTI type, I encourage you to take a free MBTI test. Here's one piece of advice for when you're taking these assessments: simply just be yourself. Don't answer based on what you think should be right. This instrument will help you affirm and clarify some realities about how you are created and possibly dispel some misperceptions about yourself and others.

QUESTIONS FOR REFLECTION AND DISCUSSION

1. How would describe your personality and temperament?

2. What's your MBTI type? How does your personality play out in school and in the workplace?

3. What factors prevented you from embracing how God wired you?

CHAPTER 9

Gifts

"When I stand before God at the end of my life, I would hope that I would not have a single bit of talent left and could say, 'I used everything you gave me.'"

—*Erma Bombeck*

From elementary school, to high school, to college I questioned whether I had talent or would amount to anything. I was just plodding through life in mediocrity and striving to compete with the cunning, smart, and talented people of this world.

For over half my childhood before high school, I lived in Seoul, South Korea, a place, perhaps more than anywhere else, where educational success equals socioeconomic status. My job prospects, marriage prospects, and self-worth were directly linked to my GPA. When I looked at my never-improving, average grades, I felt doomed. Like most of my hypercompetitive peers in Korea, six days a week—from early morning until late at night—I worked with tutors and attended the best after-school programs around so I could improve my academic performance. None of it worked. My grades didn't improve much. I still felt inadequate. I often wondered, *Will I ever be able to achieve something great?*

Deep inside I envied people who were smarter than me. I

was so fixated on what I couldn't do, and I focused all my attention on trying to hide my weaknesses. The notion that I actually had talent evaded me. I could easily name all the things I was lacking in; I felt like a bad son. I was a C student. I got made fun of at school. I was not a good speaker, and the list could have gone on.

But then I came across an eye-opening research by Gallup Organization. After interviewing employees around the world for thirty years, including more than 2 million people, they made the following conclusion: "The evidence is quite overwhelming. You will be most successful in whatever you do by building your life around your greatest natural abilities rather than your weaknesses."[1]

For most of my life, I struggled to find something I was good at. I suffered from poor self-esteem. I sometimes felt utterly clueless. And maybe you do, too. How could I be called to do something when I felt completely inadequate and ill-equipped to do anything? But in the Bible I found the answers I needed to overcome these negative feelings and become who God made me to be.

THE REAL MEANING BEHIND TALENT

The more I studied the Scriptures, the more I began to see I was feeding my self-worth from the wrong source. More importantly, I began to understand how God viewed me. In *Cure for the Common Life*, Max Lucado describes the real meaning of talent behind the parable of the talent. This was instrumental in correcting my view of who I was and how much God valued me.

Before "talent" meant skill, it meant money. It represented the largest unit of accounting the Greek currency—10,000 denarii. According to the parable of the workers, a denarius represented a day's fair wages (Matt. 20:2). Multiply your daily wage by 10,000, and you discover the value of a talent. If you earn $30,000 a year and you annually work 260 days, you make about $115 a day. A talent in your case is valued at 10,000 times $115, or $1,150,000. Place this in perspective. Suppose a person earns $30,000 a year for forty years. Her lifetime earnings are $1,200,000, only $50,000 more than a talent. One talent, then equals a lifetime of earnings. This is a lot of money and a key point in this parable. Your God-given design and uniqueness have high market value in heaven. God didn't entrust you with a $2 talent or a $5 skill. Consider yourself a million-dollar investment—in many cases, a multimillion dollar enterprise. God gives gifts, not miserly, but abundantly.[2]

Let that soak in. You're not just a number. You're not just an accidental by-product. You are His million-dollar enterprise. Let that percolate in the fabric of your heart. My friend, you are God's irreplaceable investment! How does that make you feel?

THEOLOGY OF STRENGTHS

The more you study the Scriptures, you get to see that God wants us to discover, harness, and unleash our gifts, strengths, and talents to fulfill our calling and purpose in life. Our gifts and strengths are at the very centerpiece of why God created us.

Think about it. If God is our Creator, He created us with an intention and purpose in mind. If so, He would most certainly have created us with the abilities and capabilities to do His will. The big question then is: Will we seek to discover and develop our God-given talents and abilities into powerful, effective strengths or simply focus on our weaknesses?

When you work on fortifying your strengths, you move in sync with the currents of God's streams. Everything is easier and more natural. Even if you need to become more proficient in your areas of strength, you can do so without the anxiety and self-doubt that come with struggling to learn what feels unnatural or impossibly difficult. Just coping with the negative emotions of this weakens you, sabotages your self-esteem, and holds you back from finding your calling.

STEWARDING YOUR TALENT

It's not enough to merely discover your talents and gifts. You need to act on them. Our gifts come with a holy responsibility. We need to steward our gifts.

When God gives you a talent, He expects you to use it. It's like a muscle. If you use it, it will grow. If you don't, it'll atrophy. As in the parable of the talents, if you don't use what God has given you, He will take it away and give it to someone else who will. Hence, to whom much is given, much is required. God blesses us so we can become a blessing.

I am reminded of luxury Swiss watchmaker Patek Philippe, whose clever advertising slogan is well-known: "You never actually own a Patek Philippe; you merely take care of it for the next generation."[3]

So it is with what we "own": our money, gifts, ministries, time, and our very lives.

A month prior to starting my first full-time job, I attended a seminar at my church on discovering my spiritual gifts. After a series of in-depth assessment and exercises, I discovered that my top three spiritual gifts were administration, exhortation, and leadership. The facilitator reminded the participants that our gifts came with a responsibility. As 1 Peter 4:10 (NASB) says, "As each one has received a *special* gift, employ it in serving one another as good stewards of the manifold grace of God." The seminar ended with a challenge: "How will you steward your gifts in your workplace, community, school, and personal life?"

I took on the challenge. In a few weeks, I was moving to settle down in Portland, Oregon, for work. Since leadership was one of my spiritual gifts as well as my passion, I simply Googled "Portland leadership organization." One of the top searches was the Portland Leadership Foundation. When I read their mission statement, I was blown away. It read,

> "Our mission is to strengthen and develop leadership for the spiritual and social renewal of Portland, Oregon."[4]

Not only was the organization all about leadership development, but it operated under a Christian faith perspective. I felt compelled to write an email to the CEO to introduce myself. He replied, and we scheduled a time to have lunch together. For the following four years I served on their board of directors as a pro bono consultant and leadership coach. What started as one Google search became a life-changing, profound opportunity to steward and unleash my spiritual gifts. I encourage you to take the challenge: look for ways to steward your gifts, starting right in the community around you.

———

The Academy Award–winning movie *Chariots of Fire* tells the true story of two British runners competing in the 1924 Olympics. Eric Liddell is a devout Scottish Christian and one of the finest runners in the world. Eric's sister believes that Eric's popularity has caused him to forget his promise to serve as a missionary in China. She feels Eric is putting running ahead of serving God. Liddell assures her he will return to China, but he must run in the Olympics. Here are his famous words:

> We are all missionaries. Wherever we go, we either bring people nearer to Christ, or we repel them from Christ. I believe that God made me for a purpose, but He also made me fast. When I run, I feel His pleasure. To give it up would be to hold him in contempt. You were right; it's not just fun. To win is to honor him.[5]

Liddell not only knew he was born with the gift of running, but also that he would do a disservice to God by squandering it away. Instead of immediately leaving for China, Liddell glorified God by acting on his gifts. He would end up winning the Olympic Games. What are your God-given gifts? How are you stewarding them to glorify God?

The easiest place to start discovering your calling is knowing the areas you are naturally gifted in. Do you clearly know where and when you feel alive? What is it that you feel a knack for doing? Are you a great listener or a strategic thinker? Can you motivate others to action with your words? Are you skilled at building things?

Start making a list of the things and activities that you excel in. These are often things that people might say, "Wow, you're a natural! You have a knack for doing this." What are those things in which you seem to excel? Ask yourself, "What's the one thing that I do better than others?"

The more you're able to clearly identify and recognize your God-given gifts, the more you'll find opportunities to be in your vocational sweet spot.

The truth is, we were not born with specific job descriptions taped to our backs. In *Let Your Life Speak*, Parker Palmer said, "We arrive in this world with birthright gifts—then we spend the first half of our lives abandoning them or letting others disabuse us of them."[6]

Growing up, we become a function of our environmental influences. These influences shape our expectations and more often than not try to force us to become someone else we're not. How you would respond to such external influences either helps you grow closer to or farther away from unwrapping your birthright gifts. However, this isn't the only reason why it's so hard to focus on our gifts.

GIFTS AND STRENGTHS ASSESSMENT TOOLS

There are a plethora of gift assessment tools that are helpful in unwrapping your gifts. Among these are my following favorites:

Strengths Finder 2.0 **by Tom Rath:** Gallup Research has identified thirty-four "themes" of talent with thousands of possible combinations. The online assessment takes about twenty to twenty-five minutes and generates a Top 5 Theme Report. The report is particularly useful, as it contains an action-planning guide with over fifty ideas for action.

Discover Your Spiritual Gifts **by Peter Wagner:** Peter Wagner's book is an essential read for those who want to learn the twenty-eight biblical spiritual gifts. The questionnaire included in the book is thorough and robust, helping you to identify your specific gifts. This book contains a Bible study, which makes it an excellent resource for small-group settings.

Other tools I highly recommend without professional interpretation are the following:

- *What Color Is Your Parachute?* by Richard Bolles (published annually)
- *Live Your Calling: A Practical Guide to Finding and Fulfilling Your Mission In Life* by Kevin Brennfleck and Kay Marie Brennfleck
- *210 Project* by Marc Fey, Don Ankenbrandt, and Frank Johnson
- *SHAPE* by Erik Rees

PRECAUTION: SELF-ASSESSMENTS ARE NOT DEFINITIVE

While self-assessments provide an eye-opening opportunity to better understand your natural wiring and gifts, recognize that these assessments are limited to your level of self-awareness. You might still be in your twenties and early thirties and getting to better know yourself. In fact, many of you grew up listening to what outside influences say you ought and should do in life instead of listening to our Creator and Author in life.

This creates opportunities to easily deceive yourself. Take these self-assessments with caution and don't think the results and analysis of the assessments definitively portray who you really are. But thy can help you as you pursue that understanding.

WHAT ABOUT MY WEAKNESSES?

Does this mean that I should ignore my weaknesses altogether? God uses leaders' strengths to pursue His calling in our lives, not in spite of our weaknesses but because of our weaknesses. The apostle Paul said, "When I am weak, then I am strong. [God's] power is made perfect in [my] weaknesses." While there's great value on the strength-focused approach, the Bible suggests that we should evaluate both our strength and weakness with a focus on God, not on us. As stewards, we have a responsibility to mitigate our weaknesses that might lead us into sin.

One of the paradoxes of Scripture is how God makes things happen in spite of our weaknesses. This points to the glory of God. God doesn't call the qualified; God qualifies the called. How does that resonate with you?

EXERCISE: REFLECTED BEST SELF

If you want to be objective about your strengths, you need other people to hold up the mirror. When you see your reflection through the eyes of people in your inner circle of influence, you begin to really identify an objective view of your strengths and talents. Robert Quinn and his peers created this exercise, which many business leaders and students have described as eye-opening; some even call it life-changing.[7]

Here are the steps:

1. Identify your inner circle and ask for feedback. Identify ten to twenty people who know you well from different walks of life and ask them to write a story about a time when you were at your best. You can ask questions such as, "Tell me about a time when I excelled" or "Tell me when I was fully alive." When choosing your inner circle, it's best when you select a diverse group of friends, family members, colleagues, and mentors who can paint a comprehensive picture of your strengths.

2. Find common themes. Once the feedback arrives, look for the common themes that appear in multiple stories. Make a list of the themes, the key examples that support them, and what they suggest about your strengths.

3. Create your self-portrait. Summarize and distill the accumulated information. Use it to create a brief profile of who you are when you're at your best. The description should weave themes from the feedback together with your self-observation into a composite of who you are.

4. Put your strengths into action. Create an action plan for how and when you'll utilize your strengths. Create a specific timetable and strategy around how to make this strength come alive in different dimensions of your life.

QUESTIONS FOR REFLECTION AND DISCUSSION

1. Reflect on what you have learned. What did this chapter show you about your spiritual gifts?

2. What spiritual gifts do you believe God has given you?

3. What are three specific things you can do to uncover your gifts in the next 30 days and use them for the benefit of others?

CHAPTER 10

Passions and Needs of the World

"The giants of the faith all had one thing in common: neither victory nor success, but passion."

—*Philip Yancey*

Most of the time, you will find Roberto staying past hours at the all-boys school where he works as a counselor. For Roberto, his work is not merely a job—it's his calling. He is passionate about counseling adolescent boys. I'm sure he has bad days now and then, but usually he can't wait to get up and go to work. Roberto understood how stewarding his passion was key to unlocking his calling in life.

Knowing your passion is the key to discovering your calling. For many of us, discovering passion can seem like an overwhelming task, but there are questions you can answer that will help with your quest. Grab a cup of java, open up your journal, and begin to unmask your passion by completing the following questions.

If money were not an issue, what would you do with your time?

What makes your heart sing? What breaks your heart?

What gives you energy? What drains the life out of you?

What do you want to change, upgrade, or leave better than you found it?

What target market of the population are you attracted to help?

Some twentysomething Christians mistakenly believe that if God calls them to a certain job, it will be something they detest. Otherwise, why would God have to call them to it? You might think of a country in which you never want to live and God calls you to be a missionary in that very country. This is an incorrect way to think of calling because the best missionaries are those who have a great desire and passion for the place and the people they serve.

Passions are the signposts to the path of your calling. The psalmist said, "Delight yourself also in the LORD, and He shall give you the desires of your heart" (Ps. 37:4 NKJV). Discovering your desires and passions stems from this fundamental question: What work would I do even if I wasn't paid for it?

THE DANGER OF MISGUIDED DESIRES

But desires alone can point to a wrong direction. Misguided desires, after all, are the source of all kinds of trouble. However, it can be exceedingly difficult to get in touch with your truest, deepest desires. Our motivations often become so enmeshed with our sinful and broken nature that our desires are often far from the true desires that God has implanted in the depths of our hearts.

The underlying cause is sin. Romans 7 says:

But sin, seizing an opportunity in the commandment, produced in me all kinds of covetousness. Apart from the law sin lies dead...I do not understand my own actions. For I do not do what I want, but I do the very thing I hate...So I find it to be a law that when I want to do what is good, evil lies close at hand. For I delight in the law of God in my inmost self, but I see in my members another law at war with the law of my mind, making me captive to the law of sin that dwells in my members.

For this reason, we cannot just say, "Do what makes you happy." What makes you happy—or seems to make you happy—might be far from meeting the needs of the world, or using your skills and gifts for the common good, or even from fulfilling your true desires. And the opposite is often true. The work that would fulfill your true desire appears at first to be undesirable, and it may require great sacrifice and difficult labor. And your truest desires may be met in many areas of life, not necessarily in work. Knowing what you truly desire requires spiritual maturity, perhaps more than you may have at the moment you're facing a decision.

You discover your real passion when your desires are complemented with addressing important needs of the world. Frederick Buechner said it best: "The place God calls you to is where your deep gladness and the world's deep hunger meet."[1]

When you first seek His righteousness and live in obedience, God will reveal the desires He has planted in your heart. Ask yourself, "What human needs do I 'vibrate' to?"

Your desire points you to your calling if the desire is persistent and longstanding. These are not merely passions of the moment, but rather an abiding passion that pervades your soul. When God infuses a particular desire in you as a means to fulfilling your call, your desire will usually grow, build, and evolve over time.

PASSION + NEEDS OF THE WORLD = HOLY DISCONTENT

Your passions are homing signals, calling you back to the Audience of One, the Creator who alone can fulfill every desire. What makes your heart sing? Or rather, what grieves you? What are the needs of the world you so much resonate with?

Bill Hybels calls this "holy discontent," which is "an uneasy spirit about the brokenness of this world, which aligns with the heart of God that spurs us to take positive action to change the world."[2] I believe that you cannot achieve something great until your heart breaks for God.

A number of individuals in the Bible had holy discontent:

For Moses, it was the misery of God's people.

For David, it was Goliath trash-talking his God and his people.

For Nehemiah, it was people mocking God.

Martin Luther King Jr. couldn't stand the racial oppression he witnessed in the United States in the 1950s and '60s. He couldn't stand the lynching of black people. He couldn't stand the fact that blacks had to sit in the rear of the bus. A day arrived when King could stand it no longer. He experienced holy discontent and became determined that he would devote the rest of his life to moving our nation toward racial equality. He knew that his holy discontent may very well cost him his life. And it did—one evening in April 1968 when a sniper assassinated him outside a Memphis hotel. But his legacy remains.

Or look at Mother Teresa. She couldn't stand the plight of the homeless, diseased, and destitute. Seeing their plight every day brought her to a point where she could stand it no more. She had realized her holy discontent and began functioning in solution mode. She and a few of her former students began rescuing men, women, and children who had been rejected by hospitals and who were literally dying on the streets. Bill Hybels wrote, "Mother Teresa didn't devote herself to this cause because of a fat paycheck every month; she served the under-resourced people in her midst because her holy discontent had her by the throat and wouldn't let her go."[3]

Now, if you are struggling to identify your holy discontent as quickly, it's okay. Be patient and approach this matter prayerfully. Ask God to grant you wisdom and discernment to those issues that you are addressing. I have identified three areas that I felt became my holy discontent.

1. Twentysomethings and thirtysomethings living without a sense of direction and not knowing their God-given calling in life.

2. Toxic workplace cultures that disengage employees and inhibit growth and learning.

3. Poor leadership that fails to catalyze and inspire people to fulfill their calling and leverage their strengths.

What about you? What is your holy discontent? Reflecting and articulating your holy discontent clarifies your thinking and priorities in life. It infuses passion and purpose, a sense that you are here to do more than making money for yourself and making a name of yourself. It also goes beyond the charitable and philanthropic efforts most rich people engage in, which is a noble effort, yet without answering the why, it all is vanity.

Here are a number of organizations for you to explore and research to learn more about their mission and platforms. Ask God to speak to your heart about which causes and organizations resonate with you.

American Red Cross
HOPE International
Habitat for Humanity
ONE Campaign
Charity: Water
Catalyst Conference
Compassion International
A21 Campaign
World Vision International
Campus Crusade for Christ
Focus on the Family
Your local church

Be intentional about serving in various organizations to see how God breaks your heart when you see what's broken in this world. Journal your thoughts and let the Holy Spirit do its work. When was the last time you felt you were hitting all cylinders? Reflecting and articulating what motivated you might help you identify your passion and your holy discontent. Continue to write and don't settle for the "right" answer. Give yourself permission to wander in this time of writing. Write down what makes you truly alive. When were you most motivated and felt the most fulfilled?

EXERCISE: FILL IN THE BLANK

Complete the following sentences. Brainstorm your list. Try not to censor yourself or respond in ways you think you should. Be as real as possible.

1. When I was a kid, I dreamed of:

2. I can't pass up a book or movie about:

3. If I played hooky from work for a week, I'd spend the time:

4. Most people don't know this about me, but I really enjoy:

5. I am the go-to person when my friends need help with:

6. If I could star in my own how-to TV show, it would be about:

7. If I were to make a homemade gift, it would involve:

8. I've tried it only once or twice, but I really enjoy:

9. The closest I come to a runner's high is when I'm:

Ask yourself and your closest friends, "Out of the nine sentences, which one is more appealing to me?" Prioritize your list and select the top five passions.

exercise adapted from http://static.oprah.com/pdf/passion-hexagon.pdf

QUESTIONS FOR REFLECTION AND DISCUSSION

1. Write down several desires and passions that have consumed your life.

2. What needs of the world do you vibrate to? What are some potential organizations you can reach out to serve in some capacity?

3. How would you define your holy discontent?

CHAPTER 11

Life Experiences

"So take seriously the story that God has given you to live. It's time to read your own life, because your story is the one that could set us all ablaze."

—*Dan B. Allender*

Christian apologist Ravi Zacharias once asked, "Is my life just random and meaningless strands of thread, or could they possibly be precise designs woven with remarkable care, thought, and intent?"

If you've ever watched a potter create a vase, you know that he starts with an ugly clump of clay and molds and shapes and fashions it until it becomes something beautiful. It takes hard work, patience, and a bit of muscle before the sculpture is finished. It's amazing to think that someone can take a useless heap of clay and make it into something with a purpose.

But that's exactly what God does when we allow Him to work in our lives—to shape us into someone who can accomplish great things for Him.

In Ravi Zacharias's *The Grand Weaver*, the author suggests that God intervenes in our lives and speaks to us in different ways and at different times.[1] God is the Grand Weaver who pulls each thread of our lives into a work of art that displays his magnificent workmanship. In fact, our calling can be discovered by learning to read our lives backward and examining our overall life experience—our story and themes, and people that have shaped us to become who we are today.

Zacharias recounts a poignant story of his visit to Varanasi, India, a northern city known for its spectacular and breathtaking saris that every bride wants to wear on her wedding day. Visiting a local factory, Ravi found the process of weaving a beautiful sari absolutely fascinating, as he saw how it could be likened to how God works in our lives.

Some years ago, I was visiting a place known for making the best wedding saris in the world—saris rich in gold and silver threads, resplendent with an array of colors. I expected to see some elaborate system of machines that would boggle the mind. Not so! Each sari was made individually by a father and son team. The father sat above the son on a platform, surrounded by several spools of thread that he would gather into his fingers. The son did just one thing. At a nod from his father, he would move the shuttle from one side to the other and back again. This would be repeated for hundreds of hours, till a magnificent pattern began to emerge. The son had the easy task—just to move at the father's nod. All along, the father had the design in his mind and brought the right threads together. The more I reflect on my own life and study the lives of others, I am fascinated to see the design God has for each one of us, individually, if we would only respond. Little reminders show the threads He has woven into our lives.[2]

Some of you might have pointed out your past failures and disappointments in life to God. You might ask, "How could a loving God possibly allow me to go through so much suffering?"

Discovering our calling is a function of knowing our story in life. Certain experiences happen for a reason. Our life story defines us.

Many times, I've subconsciously asked myself, "Why did I grow up as a third-culture kid crisscrossing Korea, Canada, and the United States? Why did I struggle most of my childhood adjusting to new culture, moving constantly, learning a new language? Why was I born and raised under godly parents who didn't give up on me even though I was floundering with my academics? Why did I get to live in a global cosmopolitan city like Vancouver during high school and college? Why did I experience four years of disappointment and disillusionment at a Fortune 50 company?"

As followers of Jesus, we must know that God is in control. Under His divine providence, we experience things in life that are often signposts to discovering our calling. Dissecting my life helped me understand God might be preparing me for a global calling. My international experiences has given me a cross-cultural competence and a genuine curiosity for people and things.

A perfect example is the life of Chuck Colson. His life represents a radical shift in how he came to discover his calling through an extremely difficult experience. He gained notoriety at the height of the Watergate scandal, resulting in his imprisonment. Ultimately, his experience led him to create Prison Fellowship, the world's largest outreach to prisoners. Here's what Chuck Colson said:

The great paradox [of my life] is that every time I walk into a prison and see the faces of men or women who have been transformed by the power of the living God, I realize that the thing God has chosen to use in my life...is none of the successes, achievements, degrees, awards, honors, or cases I won before the Supreme Court. That's not what God's using in my life. What God is using in my life to touch the lives of literally thousands of other people is the fact that I was a convict and went to prison. That was my great defeat, the only thing in my life I didn't succeed in.[3]

Studying your life story will help you find your life calling. Your past is one of the best signals for informing your future. Regardless of your life circumstances, remember that your life experiences happened for a reason. While it may be completely nonsensical at this moment, you'll find greater clarity and cannot deny God's fingerprint all over your life.

OPEN DOORS AND CLOSED DOORS

Be sensitive to where God has opened and closed doors in your life. While I was working at Boeing, I prayed and asked God to give me an opportunity to work for some other company where I felt I could live in my vocational sweet spot. I worked on my resume and applied to scores of companies over the course of four years. All this hard work didn't materialize into a job interview. After numerous attempts, I felt despondent. At the same time, I never saw things from God's perspective. I felt a nudge that God wanted me to pray, so I did. I applied again and again, and nothing happened. I felt God was closing a door of opportunity. In January 2015, I felt a stronger urge to step into the inevitable. I received a vision of being

Fourteen

BRILLIANT RAYS OF SUNSHINE STREAKED through the patterns on the window. They nudged Rayne in the ribs, slipped beneath the sheets, and tickled her belly, tried to get behind her lids, then settled for warming her in a bath of light.

Morning, she thought, through the haze of filmy dreams that were quietly tiptoeing away. She tried to snatch them back, but they were too quick, leaving behind only a whisper of their existence.

With reluctance, she opened her eyes, blinking against the crisscross patterns that skipped around the room. For an instant she actually felt good, her spirit light as if a long-carried weight had been mysteriously carted away during her repose.

Stretching, her body awakened by degrees: from the bottom of her feet that flexed and pointed; her slender legs that rose toward the ceiling then glided back to the mattress; her loose pelvis that did a languid rotation; the back that arched, pushing her breasts against the thin cotton gown; up to her neck that stretched the muscles against soft flesh. It was a slow, erotic dance, a ritual that paid homage to a new day.

As she looked around the room, for the first time in months her head didn't feel as if it were submerged underwater, her thoughts disjointed and floating aimlessly. A night without being weighed down by medication had given her the first sense of clarity since she'd been confined.

She sat up, a sense of the possible taking its place beside her on the single bed. She stood and walked with it toward the window, pressing her hand against the glass.

There he was. Robert. She'd thought about what he'd said to her, kept the words with her, close to her heart. She was more than this place, the circumstances that captured her. No man had ever said that to her—that she had value.

A feeling of ease gently flowed through her, settling her in a way. Her gaze followed him as he checked the manicured shrubs and potted plants for water damage.

He seemed so gentle to be a big man. Big at least by her standards. But his large hands and broad shoulders didn't intimidate. Rather, they gave her a sense of protection and comfort—that his body would shield, his hands heal.

She'd never felt that way about any man, she thought. Not even about her husband, Paul. He'd been almost gentle once, but her fears, her ghosts, her secrets awakened his beast. In a way, what they had was familiar. An ugly truth. She fed the beast.

Rayne turned away from the window. What would *something different* be like? How does it feel to love and be loved without hurt and pain?

That's the way she felt about Desi. The fleeting image of her little girl floated before her. Her baby—the only thing that anchored her, let her know that there was goodness in her. She knew what love was when she held her baby, when Desi ran to her at the end of the day, held her hand, and told her a secret. With Desi's death her capacity to feel vanished. Yes, she knew a kind of love because of her child. But never a woman-and-man love. Never that.

Perhaps all she could evoke in a man is the beast, the rage. But she believed that there was something deep inside of her that knew she could be so much more. She could care. She could love. She was worthy.

But she was afraid. Afraid to reach out and try, only to discover that what seemed new was only more of the same. To discover that would be more than she could bear.

Perhaps Robert would show her some things today—how to make things grow, to find a way to care again. She wanted to—today. She role in your upbringing. What recurring themes do you notice? Is there anything missing from this story that you overlooked?

Going through this exercise helps you see what it's really like to be on the other side of you. It reveals your personality, talent, and passions and opens door and closes doors, which shape a beautiful narrative God is writing in your life.

This process might require you to muster the courage to bring back painful memories you've hidden under the secret chambers of your mind. It's not easy. However, ask for encouragement and prayer as you seek to gain greater clarity around who you are and how God has shaped your story. In our story, we discover our calling.

Develop Your Calling Statement

Without personality, I'm constantly living under a façade of inauthenticity. Without gifts, I'm passionate but useless. Without passions, I'm uninspired to take action. Without experiences, I'm operating outside of God's story. With all present, I'm in the sweet spot God has for me.

Once you have developed clarity around these different areas of your life, I suggest you start creating a calling statement for your life.

Creating a calling statement doesn't happen overnight. It takes deep introspection, careful expression, and thoughtful analysis and often requires you to rewrite it. Consider it a living, breathing document. Don't be surprised if it takes you at least a few weeks or even months before you feel it fully captures your calling. It truly is a lifelong process.

My own calling statement reads: "To equip Christian leaders to discover their God-given calling and empower them to rise to the top."

QUESTIONS FOR REFLECTION AND DISCUSSION

1. How have your early life experiences shaped your life?

2. What are the open doors and closed doors in your life?

3. Write down your calling statement.

PART V

WHY WORK?

CHAPTER 12

Thinking about Legacy

"Carve your name on hearts, not tombstones. A legacy is etched into the minds of others and the stories they share about you."

—*Shannon L. Alder*

My grandma was affectionately known as "Mrs. Hospitality." She spent her entire life tirelessly serving others. She would spend countless hours serving guests in her house who had no place to stay. She would spend hours praying for her neighbors and prepare tailored gifts for them. In the middle of April 2015, my grandma passed away suddenly and unexpectedly. The night she died, she had just turned eighty. If one of her goals were to live a life of service, she certainly proved it through her tireless actions. She left behind a lifelong legacy of service, care, and love.

My grandma's passing caused me to ask challenging questions: What legacy will I leave behind? Is my calling crystal clear? Do I keep it foremost in my daily, weekly, and monthly planning? Does my legacy drive my everyday actions and decisions? Do I ever find myself exchanging what I want most of all for what I am infatuated with in the moment?

When you envision your legacy, you create a sense of urgency. You don't just settle by discovering your calling but by making measurable changes to live out your calling. Like Stephen Covey said, you must "begin with the end in mind," which means to begin today with the image of the end of your life as a frame of reference. Everything else is examined in this light.

The key is being intentional in visualizing who God wants you to be. Thinking about your legacy helps you to not only simply recognize the elements of your vocational sweet spot, but continue to live in your sweet spot 24/7. Instead of being empowered by other people and circumstances, calibrate your mind to the will of God by thinking through what your sweet spot looks for the next ten, thirty, fifty years.

Creating a habit of focusing on your legacy helps you strike a balance between a daily focus with a long-term perspective. Living in your sweet spot requires you to hold the compass on one hand and the clock on the other. Knowing the elements of your vocational sweet spot helps you think about the various activities and appointments in your life, while not forgetting the orienting vision and legacy you want to leave behind. Perhaps this is why Paul writes in Galatians 6:9 (NIV), "Let us not become weary in doing good, for at the proper time we will reap a harvest if we do not give up." We faint or become weary and quit when we lose sight of our vision in life. The psalmist gives us wise words: "Teach us to number our days, that we may gain a heart of wisdom" (Ps. 90:12 NIV).

THE MAN WHO CHANGED HIS LIFE AFTER
READING HIS OBITUARY

In the late nineteenth century, Alfred Nobel, the inventor of dynamite, was reading the newspaper one morning when, to his utter astonishment, he read his own obituary. The obituary was printed by mistake when it was his brother who had died. The obituary read, "The merchant of death is dead." The title was "The Dynamite King (The Weapon Maker)." The great industrialist had made an immense fortune from explosives. Alfred was shocked to see that this was how the world saw him. This wasn't how he wanted to be remembered. This misprint led him to establish the Nobel Foundation. Today, Nobel isn't remembered as a merchant of death, but as the founder of the Nobel Prize and a great humanitarian. Reading his own obituary turned his life upside down and gave him the opportunity to change his legacy.[1]

EXERCISE: WRITING YOUR OWN OBITUARY

Although it sounds a bit morbid, writing your obituary can be an excellent wake-up call to begin with the end in mind. Again, this forces you to think on the fundamental questions of life and points to your God-given calling.

1. Write an obituary as a true account of your life to date. Ask yourself questions such as the following:

   - If I died today, would I die fulfilled and happy?

   - Am I satisfied with the direction in which my life is headed?

   - Do I believe this direction is where God has intended?

   - How do I feel about the legacy I'm leaving behind?

   - What's missing from my life?

   - What do I need to do in order for my obituary to be "complete"?

2. Then, write another obituary of your ideal state. In other words, write your obituary as if you have discovered and lived out your calling in life, as if you have fulfilled the purpose for which you were created.

3. Share this with your family, friends, and church community. What does this exercise tell you? What changes do you need to make so that you can "live up" to your ideal obituary?

Without understanding your end goal, it is all too easy to become discouraged and distracted. When you forget what life is all about, it is easy to get caught up in the world's definition of success. Soon you start thinking that success is measured by material things, by power, or by fame. But when you begin with the end in mind, you can make proper decisions as you rewind back to the present.

QUESTIONS FOR REFLECTION AND DISCUSSION

1. Visually paint a picture of how you see yourself in the next twenty to thirty years.

2. How would you like to be remembered?

3. What is distracting you to develop a mindset of legacy?

CHAPTER 13

Redeeming Work

"Whatever you do, work at it wholeheartedly as though you were doing it for the Lord and not merely for people."

—*Col. 3:23* ISV

I'm a *Dilbert* fan. *Dilbert*, which appears in more newspapers than any other comic, represents how many Americans view work. Dilbert, the quintessential worker, finds his work utterly meaningless and unsatisfactory. Trained as an engineer, he finds his coworkers absolutely annoying and permanently stuck in a cubicle. Dilbert's colleague Wally illustrates many coworkers I've encountered at work. Their sole purpose is to do as little as possible on the job without getting fired.

Like Dilbert, I felt like my nine-to-five at work was a rat race. The treadmill. The old grind. *Surely*, I thought to myself, *God must have something better in mind for my life.*

Have you ever felt that you are a tiny cog in the machine? A mindless zombie?

Have you ever felt that Sunday worship has little or no relevance to the forty-hour workweek? Sadly, I'm not the only one who feels that way. Today, we are living in a world where the greatest epidemic we face at work is sheer disengagement.

Twentysomething Christians often view worship as something

reserved just for Sundays when we listen to the pastor's sermon and sing worship songs. We check off the box and we move on. On Monday, we become employee first, Christian second. We often compartmentalize our lives instead of living holistically. We resort to becoming a Sunday Christian.

In 2013, Gallup studies indicated an average of only 13 percent of people like their jobs worldwide. In other words, almost nine out of ten people either dislike or hate their jobs.[1]

You might be working in an entry-level job that seems exceedingly tedious. Without the prospect of weekends and vacations, life at work seems unbearable. At the same time, the idea of unemployment would be incomprehensible. Working for an organization ultimately provides a sense of security and identity.

More ambitious and career-driven twentysomethings may view their jobs as a tool to accelerate their way to success. They do everything it takes to climb up the ladder faster, and their lives become all about networking and building the perfect resume. Long hours of work are thought of as a boast.

It's important to understand why we work in the first place. An average American works over ten years throughout his or her lifetime.[2] Why do we work in the first place? Do we work to make a living or do we live to work? Is work disguised as a curse for human beings, a necessary evil? Or should we count work among our many blessings from God? Can our workplace be one of the key places that God places Christians in the mission field?

REDEEMING WORK: A BIBLICAL VIEW OF WORK

In order to know why work is important, we must understand the history of work. Work starts with God. The beginning of the Bible says, "In the beginning God created the heavens and the earth." Here we are immediately introduced to God, the first worker. Notice that God is a working God. In fact, the Hebrew word for *work* is used 167 times in the Old Testament, which is translated as "occupation," "work," or "business."

The culmination of God's creation is us, humankind—the crown of His creation. God says,

> "Let us make humankind in our image, according to our likeness; and let them have dominion over the fish of the sea, and over the birds of the air, and over the cattle, and over all the wild animals of the earth, and over every creeping thing that creeps on the earth." So God created humankind in his image, in the image of God he created them; male and female he created them. And God blessed them, and God said to them, "Be fruitful and multiply, and fill the earth and subdue it; and have dominion over the fish of the sea and over the birds of the air and over every living thing that moves upon the earth." (Gen. 1:26–28 NRSV)

Here is mankind's first job description given by God. We are image-bearers of God; our purpose is to mirror our Creator. Since it's in God's nature to work, we were also created with work in mind. In fact, we were called to be God's co-workers. In our work, we display God's glory, workmanship, and creativity to this world. Therefore, anyone who denies the value of work is in a fundamental violation of God's creation for humankind. Throughout the Bible, we see praises to the wise for their diligence and the fools for their laziness. Therefore, work is not simply a means to make our ends meet, nor a shortcut to achieving the American Dream; rather, it is a gift from God to honor His calling in our lives. We must understand that our work, our calling, is something that is already chosen and called from God instead of something we choose for ourselves. From the beginning, God intended and created human beings as his junior partners in the work of bringing His creation to fulfillment.

The Hebrew word for work is *avodah*, "to cultivate." In the Old Testament, *avodah* not only meant work, but also worship. "As for me," Joshua says, "I will *avodah*. I will work for, and worship, the Lord." This is a powerful image to think that the word for "working in the fields" is the same word used for worshiping the God of Abraham, Isaac, and Jacob.

In his study on work in the gospels, Os Hillman points out that "of Jesus' 132 public appearances in the New Testament, 122 were in the workplace. Of the 52 parables Jesus told, 45 had a workplace context."[3] Jesus never addressed the sacred and secular divide because such a divide never existed in Jewish thinking. The Jews understood that everything they did in work and in the synagogue was to be done to God's glory. This is why quality is so important to Jewish workers. They are not working solely for themselves, but also as worship to God.

Your work is as much about your connection with God as it is the physical or intellectual activity at the time. For example, you can be just as connected to God when working as a server in a restaurant as when working as a volunteer in a street kitchen.

If we embrace this perspective of work, why are so many people disengaged at work? Why is work so hard? Why doesn't it feel natural? Why do we feel utterly meaningless?

Sixteen

"THANK YOU . . . FOR TODAY," RAYNE softly murmured, hoping that he could hear her thoughts. She rose from her crouched position near the trimmed hedges.

"I enjoyed it." Robert wiped his hands on the fabric of his jeans, his dark brown face glistening with perspiration.

The air grew cooler. The time between them had passed. For now.

"I should . . . go back." Rayne tucked her journal under her arm. *They'll come for you if you don't,* the voice whispered. Her eyes darted quickly around the grounds, imagining the guards bearing down on her, dragging her back to her room, humiliating her. She didn't want that, didn't want the reality of her existence to crowd out her fantasy.

Robert glanced at his watch. "Visiting hours."

Say something, girl. Don't just run away. Speak up! "Your father . . . will you see him?" she asked, the words coming from some faraway place.

"I should. Sometimes he knows I'm there." He looked away.

The cape of his sadness hung on her shoulders. She wanted to say something, do anything to lift the weight. But how could she when she still could not rid herself of her own burdens?

Helpless. Again.

Rayne reached out to touch his cheek, wipe away the lines of worry from beneath his eyes, but stopped halfway when he looked back at her.

The brackets around his mouth softened as he smiled. "Maybe tomorrow. If the weather holds up, how about if we meet by the bench after lunch?"

She didn't want to feel hope, that warm glow of maybe, but she did.

Robert smiled outright. "It should be good and hot by then. I'll be sure to bring plenty of water."

Rayne studied him for one slender moment, memorizing their day together, then turned and hurried toward the entrance.

Robert watched her until she was gone. There was so much about her that he wanted to know. He wanted to find out her favorite color, places she'd been, her fondest memory. He wanted to know who she was before she came to Cedar's, who she could be when she left. And as much as he tried to deny it, he wanted to be there for her when she did. She challenged him in ways she was totally unaware of. In her, he could perhaps redeem himself. Do for her what he was unable to do for his mother and sister. Maybe.

He bent down and picked up his shears, rose, and looked out across the grounds. His men were packing up, heading home. The hospital staff escorted some of the patients back inside. Others found their own way.

Everyone had a destination. He looked up at the building. Lights began to twinkle in the windows.

Where did he have to go and to whom? Nowhere, and to no one.

How long had it been this way? he questioned, moving toward his van.

For the most part, his work kept him satisfied, fulfilled in a way. He tried not to think about the other things. His mother. His father. His sister.

He opened the door, got in behind the wheel, turned on the engine.

His mother. Lena Parrish was the kind of mother any child would want. All his friends said so, for as long as he could remember . . .

"Your mom is cool, man," Mike, Robert's best friend, was saying as they walked home from school.

I've seen too many type-A millennials resort to careerism. Jobs in investment banking and consulting are often viewed as the ultimate job millennials should strive for. Your entire life becomes centered on work.

One of my closest friends during business school now works at the nation's top consulting firm. He prided himself on the one hundred or more hours he invested every week. However, after a two-year stint, he began to see his body fall apart. He started getting sick and found himself vomiting in the middle of work. The stress was overwhelming. After seeing the doctor, he was strongly advised to take a leave of absence from his work. This time away from work was incredibly hard for my friend. His entire sense of identity came from his work, and he felt useless when he wasn't able to work anymore at his will. I believe my friend is just one of the many Millennials who suffered careerism.

In Jesus's parable of the rich fool found in Luke 12, we are warned about the peril of a life in the absence of God, one that exclusively worships work and personal comfort. Jesus says in death, the rich fool left his work and all he had amassed behind, and God said to him, "Fool! This night your soul is required of you, and the things you have prepared, whose will they be?" (Luke 12:20 esv).

Numerous studies indicate the linkage between working overtime and increased danger in general health, increased injury rates, more illnesses, and increased mortality.[5]

Speaking to a secular audience on MSNBC's *Morning Joe* show, Tim Keller offered the following advice on work, careers, and success:

> When you make your work your identity...if you're successful it destroys you because it goes to your head. If

you're not successful it destroys you because it goes to your heart—it destroys your self-worth. [Faith in Christ] gives you an identity that's not in work or accomplishment, and that gives you insulation against the weather changes. If you're successful, you stay humble. If you're not successful, you have some ballast...Work is a great thing when it is a servant instead of a lord.[6]

In hindsight, my propensity for a work-centric life was heavily influenced by my dad. My dad epitomized a consummate businessman. His sharp business acumen served him well. He rose to the top of the corporate ladder. His executive position required extraordinary responsibility and sacrifices. An average twelve-hour day would not be considered unusual. This led him to miss our family dinners many nights. Before my dad retired, I viewed my dad more as the CEO than a dad. Even my relationship with him sometimes felt like an employer-employee relationship. His demeanor as a leader at work permeated into the household at times. In high school, I missed the presence of my dad. In fact, I held a grudge against him and resolved to never become a dad like him. Only in the last several years had I confronted my true feelings and shared the pernicious impact and wound and pain I experienced due to his lack of presence.

As we canvass the landscape of work, it raises questions: What does it mean to practically glorify God through our work? How do we become an ambassador of Christ in the most spent domain in our life? How do we become salt and light of this world?

QUESTION FOR REFLECTION AND DISCUSSION

1. How do you view work, as a curse or a gift?

2. When have you experienced disengagement at work? What were some of the causes?

3. What does it mean to redeem work in your life?

CHAPTER 14

How to Glorify God at Work

"There may be no better way to love your neighbor, whether you are writing parking tickets, software, or books, then to simply do your work. But only skillful, competent work will do."

—*Tim Keller*

The apostle Paul knew what it took to glorify God at work. His secret? "Whatever you do, work at it with all your heart, as working for the Lord, not for human masters" (Col. 3:23 NIV).

We must never lose sight of who our true boss is. The ultimate boss that we work for is not a mean, Hitler-like megalomaniac. Rather, our boss is the Author and Creator of the universe. When we realize we work before God, the Audience of One, work takes on another level of meaning and significance. Proverbs 16:3 (ESV) says, "Commit your work to the LORD, and your plans will be established." We have nothing to prove when we work for the Audience of One. This radically transforms our perspective on how we see work. In light of this understanding, we can give a warm smile to our colleagues who might be annoying, frustrating, and excruciating.

Martin Luther, the pioneer of the Protestant Reformation, said you can "milk cows to the glory of God."[1] You can clean toilets to the glory of God. What matters is your prevailing attitude that says, "God, I'm doing it as if I'm doing it for you." For example, let's say you make beds in a hotel; you are probably going to make them nicer if you think, "I'm doing this as if Jesus were going to sleep in this bed."

This attitude is countercultural. It's like a refreshing fragrance or aroma. People can smell it. They can see the difference in you. When you are rooted in the Word and allow the Holy Spirit to direct your life, your life becomes an inspiration for others and transforms work into eternal significance.

A story is told in which a traveler in Europe meets three workers. A traveler was making his way through Europe as the great cathedrals were being built, and one day he met three workers. He asked the first one, "What are you doing?"

The worker replied, "I'm cutting stone."

Later the traveler put the same question to the next worker he met: "What are you doing?"

The next worker answered, "I'm cutting stone so that I can provide for my family."

Finally, later in the day, the traveler asked the third worker, "What are you doing?"

The third worker beamed. "I'm making a great cathedral."

Many of us might be like the first two workers. We focus on the immediate benefits of our work. But we occasionally find the last worker, who understands the big picture. He knows that his work is his calling. Changing your perspective makes an incredible difference! Work is an act of worship.

If you are looking for practical steps, the following are three ways you can be the salt and light of the world.

1. SHOW YOUR LOVE AT WORK

Jesus says, "Love your neighbor as yourself." This is the second greatest commandment. On the surface, loving at work sounds rather strange. You might not often think that your number one priority at work is to love your colleagues. It's hard to imagine how to apply this commandment in a workplace where talking about religion is taboo.

Loving your co-workers means that you have their best interests at heart. Love is fighting for the highest possible good in the people in which you engage with. Love is more than the conventional "rah-rah" where you simply encourage and praise others. It also means bringing in challenge when necessary because you truly want the very best for the other person. Knowing how to calibrate support and challenge is the essence of love. If you're a teacher, seek the very best in your students. Sometimes this means telling the hard truth but in a loving way. If you're a manager, seek to tap into the maximum potential in your employees. Provide constructive feedback in a way that shows you are *for* them, not only for yourself. So what does loving others at work really look like?

Tim Sanders highlights three ways to show love in the workplace in his bestselling book, *Love Is the Killer App*: share your knowledge, share your network, and share your compassion.[2] I share my thoughts on these ways to show love at work below.

Share Your Knowledge

It sounds simple. But sharing your knowledge is an expression of love. You cannot give what you don't possess. Learning is a lifelong pursuit that enables us to be resourceful. For example, if one of your fellow employees is considering leasing a car for the first time, you might pass on information on the pros and cons of leasing versus purchasing. If a new hire in your department is struggling to learn the content of your work, either give him a book or direct him to the right resource. If a colleague is struggling with navigating Microsoft Excel, you can schedule a short tutorial or even hold a short workshop for others who are struggling. Whenever you have knowledge, share it openly and generously. Become a walking encyclopedia so you can provide insight to people who need it most.

Share Your Network

According to a report from ABC 7 News, 80 percent of today's jobs are landed through networking.[3] Millennials are spending an excessive number of hours perfecting their resume when much of the time could be better spent building authentic relationships. Resumes and cover letters are important, but they are merely foundational. Rather, the key is building connections with a focus on the other over yourself. Your number one objective should be asking yourself: How can I connect this person to someone else I know who might be of help and service? Freely give what you have freely received. When you are generous with your connections, this is another expression of practical love. Just imagine the world if we start sharing our networks with other people. If one of your employees needs help with building a social media presence for your company, look around your network to see who would be a good person to refer them to and introduce them.

Share Your Compassion

In my years in corporate America, I once met an executive who I think was never trained to smile. He had an immutable poker face. He came across as extremely professional and highly unlikable. The world of work tells us that we cannot truly be who we are. Showing our emotions is a sign of weakness. Rather, the world shouts that we ought to maintain a poker face and put on the mask of professionalism, but this comes at the expense of losing our soul. Fundamentally, all business hinges on human interaction, so why resist being human? Instead, ask yourself, "What would Jesus do?" Simply showing warmth, concern, and interest to those you interact with at work is a way to love your neighbor. The greatest gift you can give is your vulnerability. When you go past your wall of self-preservation, you create a greater ability to connect on a deeper level and have long-term influence.

2. DO EXCELLENT WORK

We live in a world where when you put the word *Christian* before anything—Christian band, Christian movie, Christian art—there is a connotation that the work is subpar. It has almost become a joke. We are losing souls not because of our Christian principles and beliefs, but because of the negative perception that Christian work is inferior compared to secular mainstream work. The point is that not everything we do needs to be overtly Christian. Rather, whenever we do our work with excellence, we glorify God by being faithful stewards of God's resources and opportunities He's given in our lives. We ought to do everything as unto God, not man, and to do it in the name of Christ. Excellence is the best marketing tool to showcase Christ in our work.

A story is told of Alexander the Great, one of the greatest military generals who ever lived. One night during a campaign, he couldn't sleep and left his tent to walk around the campgrounds. He came across a soldier asleep on guard duty. The penalty for falling asleep on guard duty was instant death. As the soldier began to wake up, Alexander approached the young soldier. Recognizing who was standing in front of him, the young man feared for his life. "Do you know what the penalty is for falling asleep on guard duty?" Alexander asked the soldier.

"Yes, sir," the soldier responded in a quivering voice.

"Soldier, what's your name?" demanded Alexander.

"Alexander, sir."

Alexander repeated the question: "What is your name?"

"My name is Alexander, sir," the soldier repeated.

A third time and more loudly Alexander asked, "What is your name?"

A third time, the soldier meekly said, "My name is Alexander, sir."

Alexander then looked the young soldier straight in the eye. "Soldier," he said with intensity, "either change your name or change your conduct."[4]

As Christians, we are like the young soldier. We have a model to follow—Jesus Christ. We ought to fashion every aspect of our lives around Him.

Another modern day example of excellence comes from the hip-hop world. His name is Lecrae. Lecrae is probably the hottest Christian artist alive right now. Crowned as the "new hip-hop king," he's been invited to birthday parties for Billy Graham and

Michael Jordan and appeared on NBC's *Tonight Show Starring Jimmy Fallon*. What makes Lecrae a modern-day Daniel is his influence in both Christian circles and the secular mainstream world. His album *Anomaly* hit number one on the *Billboard* chart, which was a first for a gospel album and only the fifth for a Christian album. I believe people appreciate Lecrae, first and foremost, because of his excellence. Like Proverbs 22:29 (NIV) says, "Do you see someone skilled in their work? They will serve before kings; they will not serve before officials of low rank."

3. GOD WANTS YOU TO WORK HARD

When Jesus becomes your boss, the definition of work takes on a deeper meaning and significance. Here's what the apostle Paul had to say about the importance of working hard in both ministry and non-ministry work settings:

> You yourselves know that these hands ministered to my necessities and to those who were with me. In all things I have shown you that by working hard in this way we must help the weak and remember the words of the Lord Jesus, how he himself said, "It is more blessed to give than to receive." (Acts 20:34–35 ESV)

> For you yourselves know how you ought to imitate us, because we were not idle when we were with you, nor did we eat anyone's bread without paying for it, but with toil and labor we worked night and day, that we might not be a burden to any of you. It was not because we do not have that right, but to give you in ourselves an example to imitate. (2 Thess. 3:7–9 ESV)

As demonstrated in these verses, Christians should be known for their work ethic.

The prominent evangelist D. L. Moody was known for saying that he never met a lazy Christian. I believe that a slothful Christian is an oxymoron. And the book of Proverbs warns against laziness in the following verses:

- "Whoever is slothful will not roast his game, but the diligent man will get precious wealth" (Prov. 12:27 ESV).
- "Slothfulness casts into a deep sleep, and an idle person will suffer hunger" (Prov. 19:15 ESV).
- "I passed by the field of a sluggard, by the vineyard of a man lacking sense" (Prov. 24:30 ESV).

RECLAIMING THE SEVEN MOUNTAINS OF CULTURE

In 1975, two titans in the Christian world met for the first time. Bill Bright, founder of Campus Crusade for Christ, and Loren Cunningham, founder of Youth with a Mission, both happened to be in Colorado. The day before they met, God simultaneously gave each of these leaders a message to give to another. That message was that if we are to impact and transform America and nations for Jesus Christ, then we would have to influence the seven spheres, or mountains, of society that shape the culture of a nation. These seven mountains include family, religion, government, business, media, arts and entertainment, and education. About a month later, another key leader, Francis Schaeffer, was given a very similar message from God. It became clear that God was showing these leaders where the battlefield was.

Before ascending to Heaven, Jesus commissioned the twelve disciples to "Go there and make disciples of all nations…" After thousands of years, Christians have made disciples *in* nations but not *of* nations. Now, that is a stark difference. Growing up, I always thought that my only role in the world as a Christian is to save other people. Personal salvation. In fact, I've heard it over and over from church that my job as a Christian is to invite people into a personal relationship with Jesus. Although all of this is true and important, that's not the only thing that matters. Despite the powerful revivals this nation has experienced over the last two milleniums, such as the outpouring of the baptism of the Holy Spirit at Azusa Street and the Charismatic Renewal, few of them have had an enduring effect upon nations. In fact, we have seen nations become progressively ungodly, and Christians have been losing ground and influence in global culture.

Many Christians have retreated to the cocoon of a safe Christian inner circle. Like the spiritual monks in the Middle Ages, we have cloistered together into our subculture comprised of Christian music, Christian books, Christian movies, and Christian art. Although these are all important elements, we have become so comfortable speaking "Christianese" and forget to fulfill the very thing we have been called to transform: our culture.

In fact, our understanding of the gospel may be flawed. Truthfully, at church we've heard that the story of the gospel starts with us being sinners. Once we are saved by grace and redeemed our hope is to go to Heaven. So, essentially, we are saying our job is to somehow escape this world and simply have nothing to do with the culture. This is not the entire story of the gospel. Rather it's a truncated story, a half story of the gospel.

Rather, the beginning of the story of gospel starts with creation. In Genesis 1 and 2, God gives us a job description.

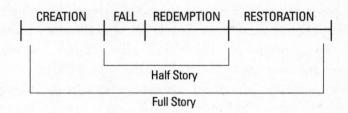

(Credit: https://www.youtube.com/watch?v=vKzjAJQapro)

In the book of Acts, the enemies of the gospel refer to Paul and Silas as those who "have turned the world upside down." This was obviously an accusation and a pejorative term rather than a compliment. The truth is that God created a "right side up" world where all animals, plants, and humans lived in perfect harmony. There were no natural disasters, sin, sickness, or death. In fact, there was shalom. However, when sin entered through Adam and Eve, things turned upside down. The world degenerated into a distorted and perverted world. The world plunged into chaos and complexity. We now lived in a cursed world and a cursed system. God calls you to turn the world right side up, to face this collision of sin and call a spade a spade. For us to turn the world right side up, we need to reclaim the seven spheres of society.

I believe a Great Third Awakening is coming. However, this wave of revival will come from the pews, not the pulpit. In fact, it will come from the Seven Mountains (think of them as "spheres" or simply "areas") of influence. The key is that those who occupy the high places have disproportionate influence to shape culture. As you consider your sweet spot, consider which place of influence God has called you to in the seven mountains of culture.

- Family
- Church
- Business
- Government
- Education
- Arts/Entertainment
- Media

QUESTION FOR REFLECTION AND DISCUSSION

1. How do you show love at work? Why is it hard to love others in the workplace?

2. What does excellent work look like in your workplace? Describe how your contribution to excellence makes an impact in your workplace.

3. Why do you find it so difficult to work hard and go the extra mile at work?

4. How has this chapter helped you redefine your paradigm of your work ethic?

CHAPTER 15

Starting Well

"Start by doing what's necessary; then do what's possible;
and suddenly you are doing the impossible."

—*Francis of Assisi*

When I was growing up, my all-time favorite movie was *Back to the Future*. Michael J. Fox plays the part of teenager Marty McFly, and Christopher Lloyd stars as Dr. Emmett Brown, an eccentric scientist who invents a time machine and places it inside a modified DeLorean. Produced by Steven Spielberg, *Back to the Future* won Oscars for best effects and best sound editing, but its greatest accomplishment may be how it affected our culture and way of thinking. What I loved about that movie was the message that everything we do now has consequences in the future.

Likewise, it's critical to start well in your twenties, considering the impact of how you spend those years on your future. And starting well requires that we cultivate strong foundations.

CULTIVATE STRONG FOUNDATIONS

To finish well, we need to start well. Your twenties is a time when you cultivate either good soil or bad soil (footpath, rocky path, or thorny bush). You must start to live intentionally by creating a strong foundation that will guide you through your seventies. Don't be disappointed by the lack of immediate gratification. A seed takes time to bear fruit (Matt. 13:3–9).

There was once a man who rushed up to a ferry that he needed to catch to get across a lake. He arrived breathless after running full steam to get there, but the gateman shut the door in his face—he had just missed the boat. A bystander remarked to him, "I guess you didn't run fast enough!"

The disappointed man answered, "I ran fast enough, but I didn't start on time." Accomplishing the most for God in your lifetime requires you to start early.

In her book *The Defining Decade*, Meg Jay calls the twenties the single-most defining decade. She notes how no other decade has the most autobiographically consequential experiences than the twenties. Consider the following:

- Eighty percent of life's most significant events take place by age thirty-five.
- Seventy percent of lifetime wage growth happens in the first ten years of our career.
- More than half of Americans are married or living with or dating their significant other by thirty.
- Our personalities change more in our twenties than any other time. Our fertility peaks.
- Our brain caps off its last growth spurts.[1]

As a clinical psychologist who specializes in twentysomethings, Meg Jay has observed how twentysomethings have considered this time as a throwaway decade, paying the price, professionally, personally, spiritually, and economically later in life. This is the biggest myth out there. No more procrastination. No more wasting your time, talent, and treasure believing you can make it up later in life.

The apostle Paul likened our life to a race. It challenges us not just to run but to win: "Do you not know that in a race all the runners run, but only one gets the prize? Run in such a way as to get the prize" (1 Cor. 9:24 NIV).

We race to work. We race to our homes, race to extracurricular activities, race to church. We race to play sports. We race here and there, and life is always full of twists and turns. The truth is, you never know what's going to happen in life. As twentysomethings, we often feel like we can't see the finish line. We feel at times like we're running around in circles. We wonder, *Will I ever make it to the finish line? Am I running well?*

COMPOUND EFFECT

The compound effect is a powerful metaphor to help you create a sense of urgency. Ever heard of the story of the tortoise and the hare? You may have heard the expression "Slow and steady wins the race." In essence, this is the big idea behind the compound effect.

Imagine two friends. Jim and Ruth grew up together. They both knew they needed to start thinking about their future. At age nineteen, Jim started to invest $2,000 every year for eight years. He picked investment funds that had an average 12 percent interest rate. When Jim turned twenty-six, he stopped putting money into the investments. In total, Jim put $16,000 into his investment funds. On the other hand, Ruth didn't start investing until age twenty-seven. Like Jim, Ruth put $2,000 into the same investment funds that yielded the same 12 percent interest

AGE	JIM INVESTS:		RUTH INVESTS:	
19	2,000	2,240	0	0
20	2,000	4,749	0	0
21	2,000	7,558	0	0
22	2,000	10,706	0	0
23	2,000	14,230	0	0
24	2,000	18,178	0	0
25	2,000	22,599	0	0
26	2,000	27,551	0	0
27	0	30,857	2,000	2,240
28	0	34,560	2,000	4,749
29	0	38,708	2,000	7,558
30	0	43,352	2,000	10,706
31	0	48,554	2,000	14,230
32	0	54,381	2,000	18,178
33	0	60,907	2,000	22,599
34	0	68,216	2,000	27,551
35	0	76,802	2,000	33,097
36	0	85,570	2,000	39,309
37	0	95,383	2,000	46,266
38	0	107,339	2,000	54,058
39	0	120,220	2,000	62,785
40	0	134,646	2,000	72,559
41	0	150,804	2,000	83,506
42	0	168,900	2,000	95,767
43	0	189,168	2,000	109,499
44	0	211,869	2,000	124,879
45	0	237,293	2,000	142,104
46	0	265,763	2,000	161,396
47	0	297,660	2,000	183,004
48	0	333,379	2,000	207,204
49	0	373,385	2,000	234,308
50	0	418,191	2,000	264,665
51	0	468,374	2,000	298,665
52	0	524,579	2,000	336,745
53	0	587,528	2,000	379,394
54	0	658,032	2,000	427,161
55	0	736,995	2,000	480,660
56	0	825,435	2,000	540,579
57	0	924,487	2,000	607,688
58	0	1,035,425	2,000	682,851
59	0	1,159,676	2,000	767,033
60	0	1,298,837	2,000	861,317
61	0	1,454,698	2,000	966,915
62	0	1,629,261	2,000	1,085,185
63	0	1,824,773	2,000	1,217,647
64	0	2,043,746	2,000	1,366,005
65	0	$2,288,996	2,000	$1,532,005

Table 1

rate until she turned 65. Ruth, therefore, invested twenty-three more years than Jim did. So over a thirty-nine-year period, Ruth invested a total of $78,000.

Now, imagine what their investment accounts looked like when they turned sixty-five. Who do you think had more? Jim, with his total $16,000 invested over eight years, or Ruth, who invested $78,000 over thirty-nine years?

It's quite surprising that Jim came out ahead. Believe it or not, Jim came out ahead of Ruth by $700,000. The secret behind this was time. Jim started earlier than Ruth. This is the power behind the compound effect.

Imagine what would happen if you started investing early on in your own life. God has endowed you with a unique personality, gifts, passions, and life experiences. He has told you to maximize what has been given during the time you are here on earth. When you realize your role is to steward your God-given calling in your twenties, imagine where you will end up at the age of fifty. You will be in a position where you will enjoy more time in your vocational sweet spot. Not only will you feel in your zone, but you are glorifying God by maximizing your calling.

REMEMBER YOUR CREATOR

We can learn the secret to starting well from the wisest and richest man on earth, King Solomon. Solomon was the wisest but also one of the most foolish. He came from a regal family. His dad, David, was a famous king. God gifted Solomon with unsurpassed wisdom, but throughout his lifetime he wasted his gifts by disobeying God's commandments. He married his wife to seal a political alliance. He acted like a pimp. He had over seven hundred wives and three hundred concubines. He forgot whom he belonged to and began to worship false gods and idols. He turned to worldly pleasures instead of pursuing God. Over the forty years of his career, he achieved great things, but he also succumbed to the temptations of a lesser man.

He regretted much of his life and said, "Remember your Creator in the days of your youth, before the days of trouble come and the years approach when you say, 'I find no pleasure in them'" (Eccl. 12:1 NIV). To finish the race, we must remember our Creator. Remembering doesn't mean to jog your memory. Rather, the verb *to remember* (*zakar*) is a command that involves a wholehearted commitment to love, serve, and fear God. Without this focus, we can become a lot like King Solomon, who wasted his life in many ways by pursuing the desires of the world.

Remembering God means putting God first. In a 2015 commencement speech at Dillard University, Denzel Washington challenged graduates to put God first:

> Put God first in everything you do...Everything that I have is by the grace of God, understand that. It's a gift... I didn't always stick with him, but He stuck with me... While you're [on your knees], say thank you. Thank you for grace, thank you for mercy, thank you for understanding, thank you for wisdom, thank you for parents, thank you for love, thank you for kindness, thank you for humility, thank you for peace, thank you for prosperity. Say thank you in advance for what is already yours.[2]

Remembering your Creator gives you wisdom to "number your days." As twentysomethings, we normally do not think about death. *What a morbid thought*, you might think. Here's what the psalmist advises: "The days of our years are threescore years and ten; and if by reason of strength they be fourscore years, yet is their strength labour and sorrow; for it is soon cut off, and we fly away . . . So teach us to number our days, that we may apply our hearts unto wisdom" (Ps. 90:10, 12 KJV).

The days we live are fleeting. The world shouts, "You're still young. Make as many mistakes as possible and learn from them. You only live once. Enjoy life!"

Sir Thomas Browne said it best: "Your time on earth, but a small parenthesis in eternity."

Live your life today as if tomorrow is your last day. Stop assuming you have all the time to make up for your time squandered away in your twenties. Start stewarding what God has given you and start being intentional. Be intentional about how you can discover your hardwiring and personality, spiritual gifts and talents, passions and needs of the world, and the message and purpose behind your life story. Ask God to use your community to affirm who you are in Christ.

Start living in your sweet spot lest you get stuck in the rat race of life.

FINAL THOUGHTS

After running several years of my life with an empty tank, God seemed to be speaking His message to me on a megaphone. It was as if He asked me, "Paul, are you going to soar like an eagle or scratch like a chicken?" The fact is, God created me to "soar on wings like eagles" (Is. 40:31 NIV). Yet, for several years after college, I felt like I was living my life as a chicken scratching out a limited existence inside a chicken coop. I was surrounded by a bunch of chickens, so I started to act like one. I began to think, act, and dream like a chicken. I began to speak up less in meetings and found myself defaulting into complacency. After a countless amount of rejections from my innovative ideas, I became passive-aggressive. After a while, I found myself drinking the Kool-Aid. I forgot my true nature as an eagle and forgot to fly.

After my college graduation, I spent several years living with unanswered questions: Is this what I am supposed to do? Why am I experiencing a firestorm of frustration, loneliness, and meaninglessness? I often wondered if I should be satisfied with the decent pay, good benefits, and comfortable living while my soul is sucked away at work. I wrestled with the fact that I may be too idealistic believing that what I'm experiencing is an exception rather than a norm.

When God showed me that life wasn't meant to be a rat race—that I was meant to break free and soar—something amazing dawned on me. I needed to be liberated. I needed to finally listen to God's call and learn to soar like an eagle.

Believe me, shifting into a life where your life is centered on your calling isn't easy. Today, I no longer work for an employer who pays me a stable salary. Instead, I'm an entrepreneur, leadership consultant, speaker, blogger, and author. Of course, I constantly wrestle with questions of uncertainty, frustration, and confusion. The existential questions I face are real. That's life. Interestingly enough, I have never felt more peaceful and fulfilled in my life.

I'm so glad I fired myself at my job before someone else fired me. Ultimately, I was doing a disservice to myself, my colleagues, my company, and ultimately to God.

Now I wake up with a feeling of immense joy and anticipation before work every morning. Following God's calling wasn't an easy decision. But when you muster the courage to pursue your calling relentlessly, God will provide.

As an ENFJ, I thoroughly enjoy making a difference in someone's life. My gifts and strengths are in leadership, building relationships, and teaching. My passion is helping young leaders unlock their God-given calling to become a leader worth following. God has authored my story such that I am able to understand people and want to help them. Not only do I feel more alive, but I get to make money doing this. As a leadership coach, blogger, and author, I am living in my sweet spot.

Why do I have to be an exception? Why can't you intentionally live out your calling? God is calling you, beckoning you to live in His presence. He is calling you to a life of significance. Live in your sweet spot. Find your quarter-life calling.

ACKNOWLEDGMENTS

This is not simply a book. You're holding a journey in your hands. I'm still walking on this journey of living intentionally toward my God-given calling and growing closer and closer to my sweet spot.

As with any journey, there are people who helped me discover my calling and live in my sweet spot. First and foremost, I am most indebted to my parents, Dale Sohn and Hae Young Lee, whose life modeled what it means to live with intentionality and in the steps of Christ. I am eternally grateful to my Proverbs 31 mom, who modeled what it's like to be innocent as a dove and wise as a serpent. I am thankful to my dad, whose humble heart, love for Jesus, and hard work reverberate in the fabric of my DNA. I have been deeply indebted to their godly wisdom and love for Jesus.

I am grateful to my Canadian homestay parents, Joan and Gerald Van Dyck, who have "adopted" me as their son and loved me, invested in me, and believed in my potential.

I am deeply indebted to my sister, Minjoo Sohn, who continues to inspire me with her creativity. Your unwavering support, love, and prayer are a source of inspiration. I am blessed to call you my sister.

I am deeply indebted to my rock-star literary agent, Cassie Hanjian, who championed the vision of *Quarter-Life Calling*. I am grateful to partner with FaithWords and work with my brilliant editor, Virginia Bhashkar, on this book project. Most important, I want to thank my Author and Creator of Life, who has called me to live for Him, by Him, and through Him. I resolve to live with crescendo as your humble servant.

Soldier on.

NOTES

Introduction

1. "Thomas Merton," AZ Quotes, accessed September 14, 2015, http://www
.azquotes.com/quote/856466.
2. Os Guinness, *The Call: Finding and Fulfilling the Central Purpose of Your
Life* (Nashville, TN: W Publishing Group, 1998), 7.

Chapter 1: Recalibrating the Meaning of Life

1. "What Millennials Want from Work and Life," Gallup, May 11, 2016,
http://www.gallup.com/businessjournal/191435/millennials-work-life
.aspx.
2. Viktor E. Frankl, *Man's Search for Meaning* (Boston: Beacon Press, 1959).
3. Clayton M. Christensen, *How Will You Measure Your Life?* (New York:
HarperCollins Publishers, 2012).
4. Ibid.
5. Wright Thompson, "Michael Jordan Has Not Left the Building," *ESPN
the Magazine*, March 4, 2013, http://espn.go.com/espn/feature/story/_/
page/Michael-Jordan/michael-jordan-not-left-building.

Chapter 2: Whole-Life Stewardship

1. Ron Blue, *Master Your Money: A Step-by-Step Plan for Financial Freedom*
(Nashville, TN: Thomas Nelson, 2004).
2. Bill Peel, *What God Does When Men Lead: The Power and Potential of Regu-
lar Guys* (Carol Stream, IL: Tyndale Momentum, 2009).
3. Rick Warren, *The Purpose Driven Life* (Grand Rapids, MI: Zondervan,
2002).
4. Max Lucado, *Shaped by God* (Carol Stream, IL: Tyndale House Publishers,
2002), 112.
5. "Three Trends on Faith, Work, and Calling," Barna Group, February 4,
2014, https://www.barna.org/barna-update/culture/649-three-major-faith
-and-culture-trends-for-2014#.VgR5XvlVhBc.

Chapter 3: The Quarter-Life Crisis

1. David Kim, *Twenty and Something: Have the Time of Your Life (and Figure It All Out Too)* (Grand Rapids, MI: Zondervan, 2014).

2. Christine B. Whelan, "Seek Your Purpose before Your Paycheck," Acculturated, May 23, 2016, http://acculturated.com/purpose-before-paycheck.

3. Alexandra Robbins and Abby Wilner, *Quarterlife Crisis: The Unique Challenges of Life in Your Twenties* (New York: TarcherPerigee, 2001).

4. Richard J. Leider and David A. Shapiro, *Repacking Your Bags: Lighten Your Load for the Good Life* (San Francisco: Berrett-Koehler Publishers, 2012).

5. Richard Fry, "A Rising Share of Young Adults Live in Their Parents' Home," Pew Research Center, August 1, 2013, http://www.pewsocialtrends.org/2013/08/01/a-rising-share-of-young-adults-live-in-their-parents-home.

6. "Millennials: Fueling the Experience Economy," Eventbrite, accessed September 15, 2015, http://eventbrite-s3.s3.amazonaws.com/marketing/Millennials_Research/Gen_PR_Final.pdf.

7. Kate Taylor, "Millennials Spend 18 Hours a Day Consuming Media—and It's Mostly Content Created by Peers," Entrepreneur, March 10, 2014, http://www.entrepreneur.com/article/232062.

8. Audrey Barrick, "Survey: Christians Worldwide Too Busy for God," Christian Post, July 30, 2007, http://www.christianpost.com/news/survey-christians-worldwide-too-busy-for-god-28677.

9. "No Time to Slow Down," *U.S. News and World Report*, June 26, 2000, 14.

10. Oswald Chambers, *My Utmost for His Highest* (Grand Rapids, MI: Discovery House Publishers, 2012).

11. Paul Angone, "3 Ways to Cure Obsessive Comparison Disorder," All Groan Up, accessed September 21, 2015, http://allgroanup.com/featured/obsessive-comparison-disorder.

12. "Media Images Propel Women into Body Hatred," Preaching Today, accessed September 21, 2015, http://www.preachingtoday.com/illustrations/2014/may/7050514.html.

13. "Get the Facts on Eating Disorders," National Eating Disorders Association, accessed November 10, 2016, https://www.nationaleatingdisorders.org/get-facts-eating-disorders.

Chapter 4: Discovering Your True Identity

1. *Memento*, Summit Entertainment. Released September 5, 2000. Based on "Memento Mori" by Jonathan Nolan.

2. Max Lucado, *Cure for the Common Life* (Nashville, TN: Thomas Nelson, 2008), 71.

3. "Nurse Records the Top Five Regrets of the Dying," Preaching Today, February 2012, http://www.preachingtoday.com/illustrations/2012/february/2022012.html.

4. C. S. Lewis, *Mere Christianity* (New York: Touchstone, a division of Simon & Schuster, 1996).

5. Leonard Sweet, *Soulsalsa: 17 Surprising Steps for Godly Living in the 21st Century* (Grand Rapids, MI: Zondervan, 2009), 10.

6. Ravi Zacharias, *Can Man Live without God* (Nashville, TN: Thomas Nelson, 2004), 173.

7. "Rick Warren Shows God's Value to 5,000 Inmates," Preaching Today, September 2014, http://www.preachingtoday.com/illustrations/2014/september/4092914.html.

8. Michelle Cederberg, "Self-Talk Tips to Help You 'Exercise' Positive Thinking," accessed September 21, 2015, http://www.michellecederberg.com/wp-content/uploads/2010/10/Self-talk-Tips-to-Help-you-Exercise-Positive-Thinking3.pdf.

Chapter 5: What Is Your Calling?

1. Os Guinness, *The Call: Finding and Fulfilling the Central Purpose of Your Life* (Nashville, TN: W Publishing Group, 1998), 4.

2. Timothy Keller, *Every Good Endeavour: Connecting Your Work to God's Plan for the World* (New York: Penguin, 2014).

3. Rebekah Lyons, "Finding Your Calling Is about Learning Obedience," Relevant Magazine, March 3, 2015, http://www.relevantmagazine.com/life/maker/finding-your-calling-doesnt-have-be-complicated.

4. Michael Maccoby, *The Gamesman* (New York: Random House, 1978).

5. Marianne Williamson, interview by Marie Forleo, MarieTV, April 2013, http://www.marieforleo.com/2013/04/marianne-williamson/.

6. Os Guinness, *The Call: Finding and Fulfilling the Central Purpose of Your Life* (Nashville, TN: W Publishing Group, 1998), 31.

7. Hugh Whelchel, "Discover Your Story," Institute for Faith, Work, and Economics, March 2015, http://tifwe.org/wp-content/uploads/2015/03/Discover_Your_Story_Hugh_Whelchel.pdf.

8. C. S. Lewis, *Weight of Glory* (New York: HarperCollins Publishers, 1980).

9. Mark R. Schwen and Dorothy C. Bass, *Leading Lives That Matter: What We Should Do and Who We Should Be* (Grand Rapids, MI: Eerdmans, 2006).

10. Jeff Goins, *The Art of Work: A Proven Path to Discovering What You Were Meant to Do* (Nashville, TN: Thomas Nelson, 2015), 139.

11. Jack Fortin, *The Centered Life: Awakened, Called, Set Free, Nurtured* (Minneapolis: Augsburg Fortress Publishers, 2009), 14–15.

Chapter 6: Demystifying Calling

1. Eusebius of Caesarea, Demonstration of the Gospel 1.8 ET in *The Proof of the Gospel Being the Demonstratio Evangelica of Eusebius of Caesarea*, vol. 1, Trans. W. J. Ferrar (London: SPCK, 1920), 48–50.

2. R. C. Sproul, "What Does 'coram Deo' Mean?" Ligonier Ministries, May 27, 2015, http://www.ligonier.org/blog/what-does-coram-deo-mean.

3. John Piper, *Amazing Grace in the Life of William Wilberforce* (Wheaton, IL: Crossway Books, 2006), 35.

4. Os Guinness, *The Call: Finding and Fulfilling the Central Purpose of Your Life* (Nashville, TN: W Publishing Group, 1998), 41–42.

5. Henrietta C. Mears, *Founders of Our Faith: Genesis through Deuteronomy: From Creation to the Promised Land* (Ventura, CA: Gospel Light, 2011).

6. Madeleine L'Engle, *Walking on Water: Reflections on Faith and Art* (Colorado Springs: WaterBrook Press, 2001) 62.

Chapter 7: Discerning Your Calling

1. Parker Palmer, *Let Your Life Speak: Listening for the Voice of Vocation* (Hoboken, NJ: John Wiley and Sons, 1999), 4.

2. William Wilberforce, *William Wilberforce: Greatest Works* (Newberry, FL: Bridge-Logos, 2007), 17.

Chapter 9: Gifts

1. Albert L. Winseman, Donald O. Clifton, and Curt Liesveld, *Living Your Strengths: Discover Your God-Given Talents and Inspire Your Community* (Washington, D.C: Gallup Press, 2004).

2. Max Lucado, *Cure for the Common Life* (Nashville, TN: Thomas Nelson, 2008), 54.

3. "Patek Philippe Launches an Advertising Film Based on Famous 'Generations' Campaign" [news release], Patek Philippe, accessed September 21, 2015, http://www.patek.com/en/communication/news/product-advertising.

4. "About," Portland Leadership Foundation, accessed September 22, 2015, http://portlandleadership.org/about.php.

5. *Chariots of Fire*, Allied Stars Ltd., 1981.

6. Parker Palmer, *Let Your Life Speak: Listening for the Voice of Vocation* (Hoboken, NJ: John Wiley and Sons, 1999), 12.

7. Adam Grant, "A Better Way to Discover Your Strengths," Huffington Post, last modified September 1, 2013, http://www.huffingtonpost.com/adam-grant/discover-your-strengths_b_3532528.html.

Chapter 10: Passions and Needs of the World

1. Frederick Buechner, *Wishful Thinking: A Theological ABC* (New York: Harper and Row, 1973).

2. Bill Hybels, *Holy Discontent: Fueling the Fire That Ignites Personal Vision* (Grand Rapids, MI: Zondervan, 2007).

3. Ibid.

Chapter 11: Life Experiences

1. Ravi Zacharias, *The Grand Weaver: How God Shapes Us through the Events of Our Lives* (Grand Rapids, MI: Zondervan, 2007).

2. Ibid.

3. Chuck Colson, "The Gravy Train Gospel," PreachingToday.com, May 2012, http://www.preachingtoday.com/illustrations/2012/may/7050712.html.

Chapter 12: Thinking about Legacy

1. Daven Hiskey, "Alfred Nobel Was Also Known as 'The Merchant of Death,'" Today I Found Out, January 3, 2011, http://www.todayifoundout.com/index.php/2011/01/alfred-nobel-was-also-known-as-the-merchant-of-death.

Chapter 13: Redeeming Work

1. Susan Adams, "Unhappy Employees Outnumber Happy Ones by Two to One Worldwide," Forbes, October 10, 2013, http://www.forbes.com/sites/susanadams/2013/10/10/unhappy-employees-outnumber-happy-ones-by-two-to-one-worldwide.

2. "30 Surprising Facts about How We Actually Spend Our Time," Distractify, January 7, 2015, https://www.distractify.com/astounding-facts-about-how-we-actually-spend-our-time-1197818577.html.

3. Os Hillman, *Today God Is First* (Ventura, CA: Regal Books, 1984).

4. Steve Yoder, "Is America Overworked?" The Fiscal Times, February 16, 2012, http://www.thefiscaltimes.com/Articles/2012/02/16/Is-America-Overworked.

5. A. E. Dembe et al., "The Impact of Overtime and Long Work Hours on Occupational Injuries and Illnesses: New Evidence from the United

States," *Occupational and Environmental Medicine* 62, no. 9 (September 2005): 588–597, http://oem.bmj.com/content/62/9/588.full.

6. Mark Galli, "Domestic Neglect: Can You Hear the Silent Screams at Home?" *Christianity Today*, November 7, 2014, http://www.christianitytoday.com/ct/2014/november/domestic-neglect.html.

Chapter 14: How to Glorify God at Work

1. "Martin Luther Quote," AZ Quotes, accessed December 14, 2016, http://www.azquotes.com/quote/898497.

2. Tim Sanders, *Love Is the Killer App: How to Win Business and Influence Friends* (New York: Crown Business, 2002).

3. Lisa Amin Gulezian, "Hundreds of Job Offered at Job Fair," ABC 7 News, May 24, 2011, http://abc7news.com/archive/8149633.

4. Wayne Rise, *Hot Illustrations for Youth Talks* (Grand Rapids, MI: Zondervan, 1993).

Chapter 15: Starting Well

1. "Our Roaring 20s: 'The Defining Decade,'" National Public Radio, April 22, 2012, http://www.npr.org/2012/04/22/150429128/our-roaring-20s-the-defining-decade.

2. "Denzel Washington Delivered Commencement Address at Dillard on Saturday, May 9," YouTube, October 2, 2015, https://www.youtube.com/watch?v=cAo0talMqqk.

ABOUT THE AUTHOR

PAUL SOHN is an award-winning blogger, speaker, and author who has spent most of his career growing organizations from good to great. Formerly employed by both a Fortune 50 company and one of *Fortune*'s Top 100 Great Place to Work, he is now the Founder of Qara, a movement to awaken and mobilize the next generation of leaders to live out their God-given identity and calling in the seven spheres of society. Paul was named one of the Top 33 under 33 Christian Millennials to Follow by *Christianity Today*. His leadership blog has been ranked among the top ten most socially shared leadership blogs in the world by the Center for Management and Organizational Effectiveness. Paul was awarded the prestigious Top 100 John C. Maxwell Leadership Award. Paul holds a master's degree in Organization Development from Pepperdine University. He's an ENFJ who refuels while in the company of others, helping people discover their God-given callings and become leaders worth following. Some of Paul's favorite things include Korean food, tennis, table tennis, travel, great cuisine, and conversations with valued friends. He lives in San Diego, California.

Learn more about Paul by visiting his website and blog at PaulSohn.org. You can also find him at facebook.com/paul.j.sohn and follow him on Twitter: @pauljsohn.